The Accidental Diplomat

The Accidental Diplomat
Dilemmas of the Trailing Spouse

Katherine L. Hughes

ALETHEIA
Publications

Aletheia Publications
Putnam Valley, NY

Hughes, Katherine L.
The accidental diplomat:dilemmas of the trailing spouse

Library of Congress Catalog Card Number: 98-74175
ISBN: 0-9639260-7-1

Development editor: Leslie Bernstein
Cover design: Bart Solenthaler
Interior design and composition: Guy J. Smith
Photo of author: Maggie Jordan

Aletheia Publications
46 Bell Hollow Rd.
Putnam Valley, NY 10579

Printed in Canada

10 9 8 7 6 5 4 3 2 1

Contents

Preface

MUCH OF THIS BOOK is based on interviews conducted with wives of American Foreign Service officers. My goal was to examine their experiences as wives who follow their diplomat husbands overseas. There are approximately 3,500 Foreign Service officers, of whom three-quarters are male. Roughly four-fifths of the men are married, which means that there are about 2,100 wives to whom this work applies. While the number of men married to female Foreign Service officers is very small, it is growing, so their experiences are touched upon also.

Few outside the Foreign Service have studied diplomats' wives. The perception exists that diplomats and their spouses live lives of ease and luxury and hence are not worthy subjects of research. Yet as one ambassador's wife said, "It was not a glamorous job," with an emphasis on the word *job*. Perhaps little attention has been paid to them because their numbers are small and their situation seems unique. However, as globalization in the private sector results in increasing numbers of Americans being sent overseas by their employers, the problem of the "trailing spouse" is becoming increasingly common. The dilemma is particularly acute for dual-career couples, whether in the Foreign Service, the military, or business. This book will show that the situation of Foreign Service spouses is parallel to that of these other spouses.

As the daughter of a Foreign Service officer, I was able to contact Foreign Service wives whom I knew personally, and I asked them to guide me to other potential respondents. (This process is generally referred to as "snowballing.") I had little difficulty compiling names of spouses. I sent seventy-seven individuals a letter describing the study and enclosed a self-addressed, stamped postcard, to be returned if a respondent wished to participate. Of the seventy-seven, sixty agreed to be interviewed. In eight cases, because of scheduling or other reasons, the interview never occurred, so in the end I interviewed fifty-two of the original seventy-seven contacted. Of the fifty-two interviewed, forty-two were wives of Foreign Service officers; the others were husbands of female Foreign Service officers, tandem couples (in which both members of the couple are Foreign Service officers), and ex-spouses. Three interviews were conducted with new Foreign Service wives who had yet to go overseas.

The interviews were face-to-face and in-depth, and consisted of mostly open-ended questions. All of the respondents were guaranteed anonymity before the interview began; therefore, the names used in this book are pseudonyms. Most of the interviews took place in the Washington, D.C., area, while a few were conducted in New York City. Although everyone I interviewed was living in the United States at the time, I do not believe that this biased the study, because some subjects had just returned from abroad and others were departing imminently. There is a great deal of rotation in the Foreign Service, and officers are required to serve in Washington at some time or another.

Most respondents welcomed me into their homes for the interview. In other cases, we met in restaurants. Some of the young mothers were delighted to get out for a meal over the weekend while their husbands watched the children. I also conducted a few interviews at the State Department, either in respondents' offices or in the cafeteria. The interviews lasted from one hour (for those new to the Foreign Service) to three hours; often after the formal interview was completed I remained, at the respondent's request, to continue talking.

The interviews covered many topics, beginning with questions about the women's childhoods and family backgrounds, and also about their early aspirations. I asked how and when they met their husbands, whether the men were already Foreign Service officers, and about the events and motives that led to their marriage. I also asked about their husbands' commitment to their careers, and about their marriages.

The bulk of the interviews usually consisted of the women's experiences at posts abroad: their role as a Foreign Service wife, the demands placed on them at embassies where their spouses were posted, the amount of time they spent in representational work, and whether they found such work interesting and fulfilling. Also discussed were specific issues related to how the Foreign Service assists, or does not assist, spouses and families, and policies pertaining to them. Whether or not each woman was pursuing, or was attempting to pursue, her own career was discussed in depth, along with the related issue of whether or not the Foreign Service lifestyle is viewed as restrictive. In the end, I wanted to elucidate the self-concept of each woman. Does she view herself as part of a Foreign Service husband-and-wife "team"? Does she feel unappreciated or demeaned as being "so-and-so's wife"? Has she forged a self-concept from roles other than that of Foreign Service wife?

My being from a Foreign Service family seemed to help make the respondents comfortable with me and contributed to the flow of the interviews. I often heard, "Well you must know…" and "You probably know this from your mother…." After I had questioned them, several women wanted to question me in an effort to assuage their concerns about raising their children in the Foreign Service.

The wives ranged in age from twenty-seven to seventy-three. Using the ages of the women and their husbands' year of entry into the Foreign Service as the most important criteria, I divided the wives into two groups whom I naturally call the "older generation" and the "younger generation." The former range in age from forty-three to seventy-three, and their husbands entered the Foreign Service between 1949 and 1976. The latter range in age from twenty-seven to forty-four, and their husbands entered between 1976 and 1990. While one wife of the "younger generation" is actually a year older than a wife of the "older generation," this way of categorizing the wives accorded with their own particular views of the Foreign Service and their role within it.

The very moving accounts of these wives are excerpted in Chapters 4, 5, and 6. Their dispositions ranged from desperate unhappiness to joyful purposiveness. While the views of these women (and of the men in Chapter 7) cannot be taken as representative of those of all Foreign Service spouses, I believe their opinions and experiences cover well the scope of possibilities. I did not set a target for the number of individuals I thought I should interview, but continued to meet with people until I had heard a range of responses and several broad themes had emerged. Many of the spouses thanked me for inviting them to participate, saying that they were happy to have had a chance to air their feelings and views. I thank them for generously sharing their lives with me.

Acknowledgments

Thanks are due to many people. First, my appreciation goes to the spouses I interviewed. I thank them for their time and openness. I am grateful to my dissertation advisor, Dr. Mary Ruggie, without whose support I could not have conducted this research. I am also grateful to my aunt, Foreign Service secretary Nancy Gamber, and my uncle, retired Foreign Service officer Daniel Gamber, who housed and fed me many times while I was collecting data in Washington, D.C. My wonderful husband, Jeff, supported and encouraged me and helped edit the manuscript. My parents, Arthur and Patricia Hughes, have helped me a great deal with this book and the thinking behind it.

My father's career in the Foreign Service gave me a very interesting early life in several different countries. My mother is the Foreign Service wife who sparked my interest in this topic. This book is dedicated to them.

The "Wife Problem" in the Foreign Service

Work and family issues are much discussed today. How can women combine career with family? How can men be more involved with family? How do children fare with two working parents? Whose career comes first? Individuals struggle with these questions as they and researchers from many different fields seek answers. This book looks at work and family issues in the United States Foreign Service, where it was long assumed that officers' unpaid wives would donate their labor to the employer. This assumption, and the policies based on it, have changed, yet circumstances continue to constrain the choices of new generations of spouses, often with painful results.

Spouses, most often wives, of Foreign Service officers are expected to serve as unpaid partners, giving up possibilities for full-time careers of their own in order to follow their husband and support their husband's career. A career in the United States Foreign Service affects spouses more than perhaps any other occupation.

A Cultural Lag

In the past few decades families have changed, but many workplaces have not. More and more married women have entered the labor force as full-time workers, so the number of what were traditionally called housewives has decreased. However, workplaces have been structured for the career-oriented male worker with a wife at home to

care for the family. Studies show that female executives
are much less likely to be married than their male counterparts, which is interpreted to mean that for women it remains difficult to combine career and family successfully.[1]
Indeed, it is a common notion that work and family issues
are "women's issues": problems that affect women, rather
than the whole society.

It is now generally accepted that women are capable of doing most jobs that men can do. Yet sociologist
Arlie Hochschild's book *The Second Shift* describes a
"stalled revolution" in the working world:

> The exodus of women into the economy has
> not been accompanied by a cultural understand-
> ing of marriage and work that would make this
> transition smooth. The work force has changed.
> Women have changed. But most workplaces have
> remained inflexible in the face of the family de-
> mands of their workers and at home, most men
> have yet to really adapt to the changes in women.
> This strain between the change in women and
> the absence of change in much else leads me to
> speak of a "stalled revolution."[2]

Hochschild points out the existence of what is often
termed "cultural lag,"[3] meaning that all parts of society
do not necessarily change together, in synchrony; some
sectors of society may not change in step with others.
Hochschild writes of the resistance to change on the part
of many modern-day workplaces that still operate under
the assumption that employees have no home or family
responsibilities, and the resistance to change on the part
of many modern-day husbands who eschew those responsibilities. Thus, some workplaces and some husbands lag
behind a major societal shift: more and more women are
engaged in full-time paid employment. One can no longer
assume that a worker has a wife at home to take care of
family tasks.

This book explores one such instance of cultural lag.
There has been resistance to transforming American women's
status and roles in fields like the American Foreign Service,

where traditional gender roles are highly institutionalized. In the Foreign Service, the traditional roles of men and women were incorporated into the organization, to its advantage. The situation of women married to United States Foreign Service officers illustrates the conflicts between changes in women's opportunities and roles, brought about by the women's movement, and traditional social structures that still constrain and direct women's choices vis-à-vis family and paid employment.

The United States Foreign Service, or diplomatic corps, was initially structured so that the unpaid family, household, and community work that women have traditionally done was important to its functioning. For instance, entertaining and influencing guests has long been a staple of diplomacy, and wives who are accomplished hostesses are indispensable to diplomatic aims, and even economic ones, as wives' skills can help promote trade between countries. The traditional homemaking and hospitality role of the wife was put to work for the organization's purposes. Yet as new opportunities have arisen for women, the Foreign Service has had great difficulty adjusting to altered social arrangements. The consequences for many Foreign Service wives of the 1990s include severe unhappiness, abdication of careers, puzzlement over identity, and lives shaped by limited choices.

There are many professions in which the wife of the employee has traditionally served as an adjunct or helpmate, including the ministry, medicine, the military, politics, and academia. (Some of these other cases will be considered later in this book.) Today, however, wives of ministers, doctors, members of Congress, and professors who choose to do so can trade in their adjunct status for their own paid work. But because of the way gender roles have been institutionalized within the Foreign Service (and, similarly, the military), and because of the mobility requirements of the job, it remains very difficult for wives to have full-fledged careers of their own. In this instance, the sphere of paid work limits the options of the employee's wife and family. Wives of American diplomats continue to be called upon to play an adjunct role when their husbands are posted overseas.

What Is the Foreign Service?

ACCORDING TO a brochure titled *A Career in the Foreign Service,* "the Foreign Service is first and foremost a corps of working professionals who are dedicated to representing America's interests—and caring for the needs of American citizens—in other countries."[4] Overseas, Foreign Service officers promote the political, economic, commercial, and national security interests of the United States. They manage embassies and consulates, carry out consular work such as granting entry visas to the United States, and organize cultural information and programs in the approximately 180 countries with which the United States maintains diplomatic relations. They may also advise American business interests overseas.

Foreign Service officers abroad report on political, economic, commercial, and social conditions for Washington, and execute foreign policy. Although, as "the front-line personnel of all U.S. embassies, consulates, and other diplomatic missions"[5] Foreign Service officers do not make policy, they do contribute to its formulation, as their reports (ideally) inform those with decision-making responsibility. In addition, much of the purpose of the Foreign Service is to create friendships in order to bring people in other countries around to the American point of view.

In contrast to the Foreign Service officer, there is no official job description for the Foreign Service wife; it is a derivative status and an ambiguous role. Foreign Service wives are unofficial representatives of the United States wherever their husbands serve. As such, they are in frequent social contact with local dignitaries. They are expected to be intelligent conversationalists and well-versed in local and international affairs. They are hostesses, cooks, employers of domestic help, protocol specialists, organizers of community events, frequent movers, students of foreign cultures and foreign languages, and world travelers. Increasing numbers attempt to hold paid jobs, and some succeed, but all serve as unpaid employees of the United States government in promoting its objectives and interests abroad.

The life of a Foreign Service wife is affected and directed by the career of her husband, more so than probably any other group of spouses. It is difficult for Foreign Service wives to pursue careers of their own, given the frequent moves that are part of the job and the continuing expectation that they will perform "support work" for their husbands. These women are their husband's "dependents" (the State Department's official name for spouses and children) in an era in which women's economic independence is championed and dependence on another for one's social role and professional and personal identity is considered unfulfilling.

This situation remains, as will be shown, despite the State Department's attempts to adjust to changed gender roles in American society. The type of work traditionally viewed as within women's special "sphere" was and is necessary to the practice of diplomacy abroad, and it has been incorporated into the very structure of the American diplomatic profession. Thus, in spite of society-wide changes, the Foreign Service has been unable to effect substantial change because the work of diplomats' wives is good for the organization. United States diplomacy is still supported by the unpaid and, in some cases, involuntary labor of many women.

The Study

I BEGAN this inquiry with several broad issues in mind: the extent of choice, the creation and evolution of personal solutions when no options are perfect, and how the decisions of some come under attack by others. I considered those women who had married Foreign Service officers in the "old" days, before the modern American women's movement, and questioned how they now look back on and evaluate their lives. For older women, who had fewer choices of paths to follow, I wondered if being a diplomat's wife offered them a more interesting and exciting life than they otherwise might have had. However, it is in the "old" days that the Foreign Service could officially require work from wives and a wife's behavior was evaluated along with her husband's job performance. Thus it is likely that the older generation of wives suffered the most exploitation.

I also considered those who married Foreign Service officers more recently, in the 1980s and 1990s, a time unequaled in terms of choices available to women. These are the women who would have been exposed to at least some elements of the feminist movement during their formative years. But because being married to a Foreign Service officer makes it nearly impossible to pursue most types of careers, I wondered if these women tend to be non-career-oriented, "traditional" women.

Is the current generation of Foreign Service wives satisfied with their lives, which allow fewer choices than are open to non-Foreign Service wives? Are they still exploited by the United States government? Are there fewer women willing to become Foreign Service wives, given their "dependent" status? If younger wives refuse to accept the traditional role of the diplomat's wife, will older wives feel that their contributions have been devalued? The situation of Foreign Service wives is a striking example of the many cases of American wives who are breaking new ground with respect to the proper place of women and wives.

Other cases include corporate and political wives. There has been significant news coverage of a spurned traditional corporate wife who argues that her contribution to her executive husband's professional success should be rewarded with fully half of his compensation. In contrast, many baby-boomer corporate wives are executives themselves, and refuse to put their careers second to their mates'. Hillary Rodham Clinton tried to expand the symbolic and social role of the political wife by lending her expertise to substantive issues, but was met with opposition and retreated.

Strategies of Adjustment

SOCIOLOGIST KATHLEEN GERSON, through her interviews with more than sixty American women from varied class and educational backgrounds, found that many of the women were leading very different lives as adults than they had imagined as children. Some who had leaned toward a domestic life were pursuing careers and deciding to forgo childbearing and even marriage, while others who had planned careers were staying at home and raising families. Gerson concludes that neither socialization nor social forces are wholly responsible for the choices women make concerning their adult orientations to domesticity or paid employment. Rather, women's motives, goals, and capacities develop and change as they move through life, so that options are negotiated and choices made in the context of changing societal cross-pressures:

> Neither chance circumstances nor individual personalities determined the paths these women took as they made decisions that shaped the direction of their lives. Their choices reflected instead an interaction between socially structured opportunities and constraints and active attempts to make sense of and respond to these structures. Constraints and opportunities in the immediate social environment limited the range of possible options and channeled motivation to select one option from among this range.[6]

This perspective views women as actors who make choices for themselves, yet emphasizes that the choices always depend on the options at hand. Everyone's position is characterized by a unique combination of possibilities and constraints. Yet for women in particular, "the uncertainties within and contradictions between the various work and family structures women confront"[7] may add up only to a lack of clear, legitimate pathways. Pursuing a career and being a good wife and mother are still viewed as incompatible in our society and by the women Gerson studied, yet choosing one or the other exclusively is also criticized. Thus for women, none of the available alternatives may be wholly satisfactory, necessitating individual strategies of adjustment and compromise.

In the following chapters, Foreign Service wives' strategies of adjustment will be examined. Because different women make different choices, sometimes they end up in opposing situations. These women, like the women Gerson interviewed, question each other's orientations and choices in order to justify their own. Young Foreign Service wives face a conflict between the constraints and demands that come with the role of diplomat's wife and the definition of personal fulfillment that precludes achieving through one's spouse. The problem is the "damned if you do, damned if you don't" trap in which neither being a traditional wife nor carrying on a commuter marriage so that one's own career is possible is considered the right choice. And combining the two is impossible. Foreign Service wives' decisions about family limit their options in society, and vice versa. For any American woman today, it is hard to perform well in both spheres, yet the Foreign Service wife faces an even more difficult predicament.

NOTES

1. See Fairlee E. Winfield, ed., *The Work and Family Sourcebook* (New York: Panel Publishers, 1988); and Nancy McCarthy Snyder, "Career Women in Perspective: The Wichita Sample," in *Women and Careers*, ed. Carol Wolfe Konek and Sally L. Kitch (Thousand Oaks, CA: Sage Publications, 1994).

2. Arlie Hochschild, *The Second Shift* (New York: Avon Books, 1989), p. 12.

3. William F. Ogburn, the originator of the term, defines it thus: "A cultural lag occurs when one of two parts of culture which are correlated changes before or in greater degree than the other part does, thereby causing less adjustment between the two parts than existed previously." William F. Ogburn, "Cultural Lag as Theory," in William F. Ogburn, *On Culture and Social Change: Selected Papers*, ed. Otis Dudley Duncan (Chicago: University of Chicago Press, 1964), p. 86.

4. Department of State Publication 9883, *A Career in the Foreign Service* (Washington, DC: U.S. Department of State, 1991), p. 1.

5. Ibid., p. 2.

6. Kathleen Gerson, *Hard Choices: How Women Decide about Work, Career, and Motherhood* (Berkeley: University of California Press, 1985), p. 192.

7. Ibid., p. 124.

2

The "Wife Of"

Until a generation ago, American middle- and upper-class married women were expected to be housewives. They took care of the home and children while their husbands went to work; their lives were determined in large measure by the husband's goals and desires. Wives were to change residence and lifestyle as their husband, or their husband's job, dictated. In marriage, as Simone de Beauvoir wrote, the wife "takes his name; she belongs to his religion, his class, his circle; she joins his family, she becomes his 'half.' She follows wherever his work calls him and determines their place of residence; she breaks more or less decisively with her past, becoming attached to her husband's universe."[1]

The roles of middle- and upper-class American women were prescribed by the mid-nineteenth century traditions of domesticity and chivalry. The separation of home and workplace that occurred during the Industrial Revolution both reflected and profoundly affected men's and women's roles and the relative value of those roles within the emerging professions. According to this ideology of "separate spheres," women's proper sphere was the home, the church, or the charitable society. The idea that women were morally and spiritually superior to men was used as justification for their confinement to the domestic world; it was argued that women were too pure to be allowed into the sordid world of politics or business.

From the early years of industrialization up to the 1970s, occupational structures were based on the premise that in middle- and upper-class families it was the husband who left the home and went elsewhere to work. At the same time, "separate spheres" relegated the responsibilities of home and family entirely to the wife. As sociologist Martha Fowlkes explains in *Behind Every Successful Man*,

> Central to the traditional system of male careers is a traditional wife at home whose roles are integral to her husband's career, and whose existence and responsibilities constitute major building blocks in the foundation of modern professional structures.[2]

Individually, the work of wives and mothers at home has been essential to the success of their husbands and sons in their work outside the home; societally, women's work in the private sphere has made possible men's work in the public sphere.

Research on the Role of the Wife

SOME RESEARCH was done on the role of the wife, vis-à-vis her husband and his career, before the modern women's movement wrought its many changes. Beginning in the 1950s sociologists, most notably William H. Whyte, Jr., began to study the situation of the corporate wife. In articles such as "The Wife Problem,"[3] Whyte asserted that corporations of the day wanted the wives of their employees to be adaptable and gregarious, and to realize that their husbands belonged to the corporation—whatever was good for the corporation was also good for the family and even the country. In those years, some company executives screened the wives of prospective employees to detect if they had the above qualities, often through seemingly innocent social calls.

Even in the mid-1970s, according to Rosabeth Moss Kanter's well-known work *Men and Women of the Corporation*, corporate attention was paid to the characteristics of wives, who "were essential elements at social gatherings."[4]

The married man was the preferred employee because he brought two people to the job: himself and his wife. Kanter found that the most common complaint of the wives in her study was that their company role was too limited. In accord with Kanter, Whyte found that the corporate wife was perfectly satisfied with the attention she received, because to her the corporation represented opportunity, benefits, and security.

Sociologist Hanna Papanek also published work on corporate wives in the 1970s, placing them within a framework she calls the "two-person career."[5] The "two-person career" refers to the situation of many corporate wives, in which formal and informal employer demands are placed on both members of a married couple when the male is the sole paid employee. Wives who lack a career of their own may be fulfilled as part of a "two-person career" as they meet their needs for achievement through their husband's career accomplishments. Papanek calls this "vicarious achievement."

A study by sociologists Eliza Pavalko and Glen Elder distinguished between types of support wives provided to husbands in the 1940s, 1950s, and 1960s.[6] Some of the wives were identified as "unpaid partners," the researchers' synonym for Papanek's two-person career. Those who fell into this category were wives of clergy, academics, and businessmen, who referred to their husbands' jobs as "our work." "Auxiliary workers," on the other hand, were those wives who provided office support, often to family businesses. The last group, the "enablers," were those who provided a variety of support services, such as entertaining and volunteer work, but had some choice about whether or not to do so. Doctors' wives were an example. The authors found that for wives who did not pursue a paid career of their own, extensive involvement in their husband's career gave them an outlet for work ambitions and a sense of vicarious achievement.

Wives of politicians are another interesting case. These women have difficulty pursuing a profession themselves, considering the demands made upon them by their husbands' profession. Their personal freedom is often limited, also. They are wives of public men, and as such they share a common position in the social structure: an ambiguous position. Officially their personalities and accomplishments are of no import to their husband's professional status; yet they cannot help but be drawn into the world of his occupation.

Joyce Schuck wrote about her experiences as a political wife after her husband's unsuccessful 1986 gubernatorial campaign in Colorado:

> When I became a political wife, I assumed that the political system would reflect the progress women have made in their struggle to achieve personal and economic independence. Instead, I was appalled to learn that the wife of a politician is expected to present herself as a supportive 'traditional' wife who stays at home raising the children, one who possesses no ambitions of her own except to dutifully subordinate herself for the sake of her husband's career.[7]

Her situation led her to interview other political wives and publish her findings. She found that "many political wives are at a loss to describe themselves independently of their husbands. They define their identities externally and passively through the successes and failures and present standing of their husbands' political careers."[8] This is not surprising, she explains, when political wives are still viewed by others primarily as the "wife of" the politician. Indeed, another political wife, Sondra Gotlieb, titled her memoirs of the time her husband served as Canadian ambassador to the United States, *Wife Of.*[9]

According to Schuck, although women's attitudes and attitudes about women have changed, the role of the political wife has not. During the 1992 presidential election campaign, this issue arose around Hillary Rodham Clinton's previous refusal to take her husband's surname, which was assumed to have contributed to her husband's losing reelection as governor of Arkansas. Then Mrs. Clinton received negative publicity when she defended her career by saying, "I suppose I could have stayed home and baked cookies," a remark that was widely viewed as a denigration of women's traditional role as homemaker. Unsure about whether the public was ready for a new kind of political

wife, one who has her own professional identity, the
Clinton team presented Mrs. Clinton as someone who *does*
bake cookies and do other things that wives have traditionally done. Since Clinton became President, there have
been numerous image makeovers for the First Lady.

It is clear from the studies cited above that wives'
identity issues are important in considering what it means
to be the "wife of." Women without their own professional identities may not only identify themselves as "wife,"
but as "wife of": "corporate wife," "doctor's wife," and
the like. Fowlkes's study of wives of doctors and of professors illustrates this point. While three-quarters of the
sample of academics' wives had their own paid occupations, only one-quarter of the doctors' wives did. The
majority did unpaid community and hospital work. The
author writes:

> Like the minister's wife, the doctor's wife has
> traditionally been expected to share in the be-
> lief system of professional commitment, which
> is thought of as transcendent of personal self-
> interest and in the service of a higher good....
> Her identity becomes an extension of his, and
> as his adjunct she proclaims his good work
> through her own.[10]

Doctors' wives may not only have a "vicarious role," in
which they achieve through their husbands' occupation,
but they may also have a "vicarious identity": their self-
esteem and sense of who they are may be defined through
their husbands. However, the role of academics' wives had
changed along with the wider society. While the older academic wives told of being "taken in hand" by the wife of
the departmental chairman when their husbands were first
hired, and were told of certain social obligations they were
expected to fulfill, this was no longer the case in the late
1970s, when the author conducted her interviews.

Studies of wives whose husbands' careers require
constant geographic moves is particularly pertinent to a
study of wives of Foreign Service officers. Military wives
are also expected to move from base to base, which iso-
lates them from their extended family and harms their job

and career prospects. Research has shown that frequent moving can be psychologically damaging, especially for the wife who moves for the sake of her husband's career.[11] Robert Seidenberg has studied corporate wives who must follow their geographically mobile husbands. He points out that

> In contrast to her husband, whose credentials are easily transferable, her identity as a person, apart from being a wife or a mother, is rarely transferable. In a new community, she finds that she must create one all over again.[12]

Thus she may have her identity in the new location solely determined by him, again, as "wife of." Because in some circles being a homemaker is no longer a socially valued identity, self-esteem problems may arise for wives who do not attain recognizable achievements outside the home.

Greater Choices for Women

As THE modern American women's movement has progressed, many women have acquired their own professional identities. Women who now have their own careers do not need to achieve vicariously through their husbands, or have a vicarious identity. Yet these changes have occurred in many cases without necessary parallel changes in occupational and governmental structures. In some occupations, such as medicine, the ministry, the military, and politics, the traditional role of the "wife of" has not changed a great deal. Thus whether a woman is able to pursue her own professional interests still may depend on the career of the man she marries.

Of course, not every wife chooses to pursue a career. Some who are economically able to do so (which may say something about the occupation of their husbands) choose to expend their efforts primarily within the home; others combine household and childcare responsibilities with part-time or volunteer work; others do desire their own professional identity. Yet the pattern a wife follows may have a great deal to do with the career of her husband.

Janet Finch's *Married to the Job: Wives' Incorporation in Men's Work* is an overall look at how a man's particular job or career affects the life of his wife. Finch asserts that "when a woman marries, she marries not only a man but also she marries his job, and from that point onwards will live out her life in the context of the job which she has married."[13] Whether a woman marries a police officer, a politician, or a miner, Finch shows, has an enormous effect on a woman's home life and career possibilities. Thus where a woman finds herself may be partially a result of constraints or possibilities posed by the career of her husband.

Of course, the causality may run in the other direction: women may choose husbands whose career and family plans complement their own orientation toward the marital role. This situation may be common, yet the point remains that many women do marry their husband's occupation along with their husband, and certain kinds of occupations will then circumscribe their roles and work lives. As Pavalko and Elder have stated, even as "occupations change and as spouses become less uniform in the willingness and/or ability to take on this role," some professions "may continue to place heavy demands on wives through frequent job transfers or expectations that they establish reputations in the community."[14] Geographic mobility requirements of some jobs, and social duties attached to others, may restrict women from pursuing their own careers, inhibiting them from creating a professional identity of their own.

Whether such wives insist on their own career is also viewed as important because of their husband's professional standing. When these women choose to pursue their own careers, they may jeopardize the success of their husband; such cases have been documented in the military. That this situation continues is due to the cultural lag described earlier: employers, and to some extent husbands, have not yet adapted to the changes in women's roles.

The Role of the Foreign Service Wife

THERE HAVE been few studies of Foreign Service spouses. One study of a British diplomatic mission in a Middle

Eastern capital found that the wives were absorbed into their husbands' roles; the author found that their collective self-image was that of dedicated wives.[15] Committees of American Foreign Service officers and their spouses have undertaken some research under the auspices of the Foreign Service itself. In a collection of essays by Foreign Service officers and their spouses, a wife asks, "But what of the role of the wife—what of my role—in diplomacy?"[16] This wife goes on to point out that the dilemma of the Foreign Service wife is that the wife herself is not the only one to define her role. This demonstrates that Foreign Service wives, or spouses, constitute a special case worth looking at. This book will describe how the role of the Foreign Service wife was first structured and how it has changed.

A role is the expected social behavior of a person according to his or her social position. Anthropologists now agree that division of labor by sex has existed in every society, albeit in varying degrees, so throughout history women have been allocated roles on the basis of their sex alone. As discussed above, from the mid-nineteenth to the early twentieth century, this division of labor by sex was known as "separate spheres"; each sex had its own sphere for which its constituents were "naturally suited." In the Foreign Service, sex was a basis for role assignment. Wives were initially allocated the roles of helpmate and hostess, as these roles fit with the notions of proper roles for women. One sociologist has written that a Foreign Service wife has a vicarious role, "by virtue of one's association with another person's role," in this case, the role of her husband, a diplomat.[17]

The diplomat has a "representational" role, concerned with the relations between one collectivity and another, in this case the United States and the country to which the diplomat is assigned. When posted overseas, every public act and word of the diplomat may be given meaning and is thus relevant to the diplomatic purpose. Clearly, this representational role will carry over to the individual's spouse. If every public act of the diplomat may be seen as symbolic, so, too, is the behavior of his wife. Whom a wife invites to the diplomatic residence for tea—or, more important, whom she does not invite—may or may not reflect her government's policies, but others may perceive that it does. The Foreign Service wife, while an "unofficial" individual, is rarely in the realm of the unofficial; thus her behavior may both reflect and affect her husband's position. However, unlike her husband's representational role, hers is different because it is not necessarily her choice, it is not part of a job description, and it is unpaid.

Representational work that Foreign Service wives perform includes planning and giving their own parties (sometimes for hundreds of people and sometimes with little notice); attending the parties of others; attending numerous ceremonies, "ribbon-cuttings," and the like; and taking part in and often organizing charitable and community activities and morale-boosting gatherings for the American community at posts overseas. All must be done with a "genuine" smile and a "personal" interest in the event. Foreign Service officers receive representational allowances (sometimes called "entertainment allowances") for such work (the amount depends on the rank of the officer), for which every receipt must be tallied and submitted. Wives often complete this paperwork.

In sum, representational work includes various kinds of unpaid work that Foreign Service wives perform to support their husbands' paid occupation. Traditionally, it has been a major part of the role of the Foreign Service wife and is seen as an extension of her traditional care-giving functions. Given the narrow roles allowed to women until just a few decades ago, it is likely that the early Foreign Service wives experienced a high degree of affiliation between role and self, meaning they did not miss having a separate professional identity.

Conclusion

THE ROLE of the wife in America has changed drastically in the past few decades. In the past, married women's personal identities were based around being the "wife of"; indeed, women were once expected to forgo any professional identity for themselves and to live through their husbands and their husbands' work. Women often served as "unpaid partners" or "auxiliary workers" to their husband's career, and research shows that many gained satisfaction, or vicarious achievement, from doing so. Foreign Service wives, in particular, have played an important role in their husbands' work because of the representational nature of the diplomatic career.

Today, most American women can choose to trade in their auxiliary status for professional status; they can give up vicarious achievement for their own professional achievement. Women have many more choices within fewer constraints. Most husbands and workplaces no longer assume that wives will be unpaid partners. The next chapter, however, discusses in greater detail the situation of wives of Foreign Service officers, many of whom not only are inhibited from pursuing careers of their own but also still face pressure to be adjuncts to their husbands' work.

NOTES

1. Simone de Beauvoir, *The Second Sex* (New York: Vintage Books, 1952), p. 479.

2. Martha R. Fowlkes, *Behind Every Successful Man: Wives of Medicine and Academe* (New York: Columbia University Press, 1980).

3. William H. Whyte, Jr., "The Wife Problem," *Life* (January 7, 1952), pp. 32–48.

4. Rosabeth Moss Kanter, *Men and Women of the Corporation* (New York: Basic Books, 1977), p. 105.

5. Hanna Papanek, "Men, Women, and Work: Reflections on the Two-Person Career," *American Journal of Sociology* 78, 4 (1973), pp. 852–872.

6. Eliza K. Pavalko and Glen H. Elder, Jr., "Women Behind the Men: Variations in Wives' Support of Husbands' Careers," *Gender and Society* 7, 4 (December 1993), pp. 548–567.

7. Joyce Schuck, *Political Wives, Veiled Lives* (Lanham, MD: Madison Books, 1991), p. ix.

8. Ibid., p. xvii.

9. Sondra Gotlieb, *"Wife Of"...An Irreverent Account of Life in Powertown* (Washington, DC: Acropolis Books, 1985).

10. Fowlkes, *Behind Every Successful Man*, p. 46.

11. Robert Seidenberg, M.D., *Corporate Wives—Corporate Casualties?* (New York: AMACOM, 1973); Naomi Gerstel and Harriet Gross, *Commuter Marriage: A Study of Work and Family* (New York: Guilford Press, 1984); Audrey T. McCollum, *The Trauma of Moving: Psychological Issues for Women* (Newbury Park, CA: Sage Publications, 1990); Anne B. Hendershott, *Moving for Work: The Sociology of Relocating in the 1990s* (Lanham, MD: University Press of America, 1995).

12. Seidenberg, *Corporate Wives—Corporate Casualties?*, p. 1.

13. Janet Finch, *Married to the Job: Wives' Incorporation in Men's Work* (London: George Allen & Unwin, 1983), p. 1.

14. Pavalko and Elder, "Women Behind the Men," p. 563.

15. Hilary Callan, "The Premiss of Dedication: Notes Towards an Ethnography of Diplomats' Wives," in *Perceiving Women*, ed. Shirley Ardener (London: Malaby Press, 1975), p. 100.

16. Margaret W. Sullivan, untitled essay in *Diplomacy: The Role of the Wife*, ed. Martin F. Herz (Washington, DC: Georgetown University, Institute for the Study of Diplomacy, 1981), p. 60.

17. Arlie Hochschild, "The Role of the Ambassador's Wife: An Exploratory Study," in *Journal of Marriage and the Family* 31, 1 (February 1969), p. 73.

3

"Two-for-the-Price-of-One": Wives in the Foreign Service

Wives of diplomatists enjoy the same privileges, honours, precedence and title as their husbands. The wife of the senior diplomatic representative of the highest category is called the doyenne. Her functions will vary widely from one post to another.... In general it may be said that her functions complement those of her husband.... Where the doyenne is herself an ambassador, however, it would probably be too much to expect her to fulfill the double task of ambassador and ambassador's wife. On the other hand, if an ambassador is accompanied by her husband, the fact that the roles cannot be neatly reversed has created many a perplexing situation.[1]

What creates "many a perplexing situation" is not perplexing at all; the fact is that diplomats are assumed to be men, and diplomats' spouses are assumed to be women. Thus the role that diplomats' wives have played for decades has been defined according to what has been considered the proper role of women in general. Despite the existence of female ambassadors today, there is no recognized "role of the ambassador's husband" that corresponds to the "role of the ambassador's wife." The following is a brief history of the American Foreign Service, which views the development of the role of the wife from a cultural and historical perspective.

According to W. Wendell Blancké, a historian of the Foreign Service, the first American diplomats were "Revolutionary representatives," men who attempted to find support in Europe for the American Revolutionary cause. In 1781 the Continental Congress created the Department of Foreign Affairs, renamed the Department of State in 1789. The first Secretary of State was Thomas Jefferson. Blancké states that in these early days of U.S. diplomatic history

> high diplomatic posts usually went to generous and politically powerful campaign contributors who, being already well heeled, felt the urge to enhance their prestige and, not always incidentally, to satisfy the social ambitions of their wives.[2]

The comment regarding wives shows that a position as a diplomat would not only give social status to the man holding the position, but also to his wife. Diplomacy was not yet a career or profession, as overseas posts went to "politicians between jobs or merchants, bankers, or lawyers on leave from their regular professions,"[3] but it is apparent that posts abroad were considered to be prestigious.

It was not until the middle of the nineteenth century that the Department of State began to institute a formal structure. Acts of Congress in 1855 and 1856 created fixed salaries for ambassadors, or ministers, as they were called then, and also organized the consular system. The 1883 Civil Service Act first established the idea of meritocratic government, whereby appointments were based on examination scores, but this act did not apply to the Foreign Service. In 1895 President Grover Cleveland issued an executive order requiring oral and written examinations for consuls, and in 1909 President William H. Taft ordered all those working in the Foreign Service under the rank of minister (thereby excluding senior overseas representatives) to be placed within the Civil Service and thus in the merit system. Examinations and the efficiency report system were introduced. A 1915 law introduced the system of assigning officers to grades or ranks, instead of to posts, continuing the trend towards meritocracy.

The Rogers Act of 1924 established the permanent career service—the Foreign Service as we know it today.

The Rogers act combined the diplomatic and consular services into the unified Foreign Service of
the United States, with its permanent officers below the rank of minister designated Foreign Service officers (FSOs) subject to diplomatic or
consular appointment interchangeably. It provided
for appointment by open, competitive examination with promotion strictly on a merit basis, established a new salary and retirement scale, and
gave authority for a system for representation (entertainment) allowances—thus putting the Service
for the first time on a secure professional basis.[4]

However, despite the "open" examination process, the
Foreign Service maintained its upper-crust identity. According to historian Martin Weil, the written examination was
of little importance in reality: "The oral interview before a
pool of Foreign Service officers was really all that mattered.
Style, grace, poise, and, above all, birth were the key to
success."[5] This author describes the "founding fathers of
the American diplomatic profession" as "members of an
exclusive club."[6] Most of those who served in the early decades of the twentieth century had been educated at prep
schools and then later at Harvard, Yale, or Princeton (and
this type of educational background is still common among
Foreign Service officers, leading to concern that the high
Ivy League representation yields a diplomatic corps that is
unrepresentative of American society). Those who came
from middle-class, non-Northeastern families who were
deemed superior enough to be admitted soon took on the
mannerisms and the "values of the club."[7]

Other legislative measures followed, including the creation of the Foreign Service Institute, which provides officers with lessons in foreign languages and other training
(1946); the institution of the "up or out" policy, which
prohibits FSOs from remaining too long in one grade, so
that they must either merit promotion or resign (1946);
and the establishment of funds for allowances for service in
hardship posts (1955).

During the 1950s and 1960s the Foreign Service suffered a crisis of confidence. McCarthyism was running ram-
pant, draining the diplomatic corps of experienced men and
damaging morale. Moreover, an influential book published

in 1958, *The Ugly American,* painted a wholly negative picture of the American diplomat. While the book is fiction, the authors claim that it is based on fact. They portray an ambassador as a blundering fool, biding his time while he awaits his appointment as a federal judge, enjoying duty-free liquor and a large, beautiful residence. He is unable to speak the language of the country to which he is posted, so he is repeatedly taken advantage of. The authors state in the epilogue that half of all Foreign Service officers do not speak any language other than English. They also argue that "too often personal wealth, political loyalty, and the ability to stay out of trouble are qualities which outweigh training in the selection of ambassadors."[8] And they criticize recruitment literature, replete with descriptions of perquisites and benefits and pictures of Americans shopping in exotic locations abroad, that was not attracting candidates with seriousness of purpose. In addition, the writers make the following charge:

> Our diplomats overseas spend a great deal of time entertaining highly placed Americans instead of working at their primary jobs. We have seen embassies in Asia which are so active in the entertainment of V.I.P.s that they resemble tourist agencies. The time spent on arrangements, briefings, cocktail parties, protocol visits, and the care and maintenance of wives leaves almost no time for the study of the local situation.[9]

The result of all this, according to the authors, was that the prestige of Americans declined abroad. With the publication of this book, the prestige of American diplomats also declined at home. *The Ugly American* contributed to a conception of the American diplomatic corps which is still with us today. If not as outright fools, American diplomats and their wives are sometimes viewed as pampered, privileged party-goers whose work (if they are actually doing any) is not at all vital to American interests. Currently there are members of Congress who believe that American Foreign Service personnel live too well overseas, and they have influenced regulations limiting the size of housing for personnel posted abroad.

Today, Foreign Service personnel come from five foreign affairs agencies: the State Department, the U.S.

Agency for International Development (USAID), the U.S. Information Agency (USIA), the Foreign Commercial Service (FCS), and the Foreign Agricultural Service (FAS). There are approximately 6,400 employees of the State Department who take assignments overseas. These include Foreign Service "specialists": communications officers, security officers, information managers and other technicians, secretaries, and medical personnel; and "generalists": Foreign Service officers (FSOs), or diplomats. This book focuses on the latter.

Foreign Service officers are typically "coned" into one of four specialties: administrative, consular, political, or economic affairs; and they have a representational role overseas. While all must agree to "worldwide availability," most are intermittently assigned to Washington, D.C. Jefferson contended that diplomats should be recalled from time to time so that they would not lose touch with the country they were supposed to be representing. At times, a strong dollar, which translates into a high standard of living overseas, makes assignments abroad more attractive to officers than jobs in Washington. It has become somewhat more difficult to send families overseas, however, partially due to the spouse issues discussed here.

Just over three-quarters of Foreign Service officers are male, and of these, about four-fifths are married. Only about a third of the much smaller percentage of female Foreign Service officers are married. Thus, wives of Foreign Service officers still greatly outnumber husbands of Foreign Service officers: 90 percent of Foreign Service spouses are women. Even within the entry-level ranks, incoming men are much more likely than incoming women to be married. This indicates that despite increased recruitment of female officers, female spouses will continue to outnumber male spouses for years to come. That is why this book focuses primarily on wives.

Women in the Foreign Service Before the Women's Movement

THE ROLE of women in the Foreign Service has been primarily that of wife. During the early decades of the Foreign

Service, the mid-nineteenth century traditions of domesticity and chivalry limited women's roles, or at least middle- and upper-class women's roles, in the United States. The belief that women had talents different from those of men was institutionalized in the early Foreign Service. It was widely stated that with the hiring of a Foreign Service officer, the Department of State was getting "two-for-the-price-of-one": the officer and his wife. The homemaking, hostessing, and charitable activities that were seen as belonging to "woman's sphere" became an extremely important part of the structure of the Foreign Service. Entertaining others has long been an important part of the diplomatic profession, and it was deemed appropriate, as I will explain in greater detail below, that such duties naturally belonged to the wife.

Although as early as 1899 some women were serving overseas as clerks, the first woman Foreign Service officer, Lucille Atcherson, was not appointed until 1922. Historian Homer Calkin notes that when Atcherson (who was, following the policy of the time, unmarried) was sent overseas, protocol problems ensued.[10] Given another author's description of the Foreign Service at that time as a male "club," this is not surprising. In 1924 Secretary of State Charles Evans Hughes stated that no woman should be prevented from entering the Foreign Service because of her sex. Still, from 1930 until after World War II not one other woman was appointed, despite the issuance of a pamphlet in 1928 titled *Opportunities for Women as Officers in the Foreign Service of the United States,* which avowed equality of opportunity in the Foreign Service. By the 1960s, there were a few hundred female Foreign Service officers, but until 1971 they were required to resign upon marriage.

Many wives become associated in some way with their husband's occupation and place of employment. Yet unlike other wives, Foreign Service wives have had an institutionalized role to play in their husband's profession. A 1965 Department of State publication declared that

> While living overseas a wife is expected to contribute to the realization of our foreign policy objectives: by creating a home environment

which enables her husband to do his work most
effectively; by representing the best in America
through her home and her children; by foster-
ing a friendly team spirit in the official American community; by cultivating personal contacts
in both the local and American community; by
participating in community activities; and by
assisting in other representational duties.[11]

These duties were required of wives until just over twenty-
five years ago; until 1972 assessments of wives were included in their husbands' efficiency reports. When
inspectors came from Washington to an embassy abroad
to evaluate its functioning, it was "part of the job to size
up wife and family, where applicable."[12]

The 1950s Wife as Foreign Service Partner

BY THE mid-1950s there were more than 3,000 Foreign
Service officers serving both overseas and in Washington,
D.C. The Zeitgeist of this era, stemming from changes in
the family and women's roles in the post-World War II
years in the United States, is well described by Betty
Friedan:

Over and over women heard in voices of tradition and of Freudian sophistication that they
could desire no greater destiny than to glory in
their own femininity.... They learned that truly
feminine women do not want careers, higher
education, political rights.... All they had to do
was devote their lives from earliest girlhood to
finding a husband and bearing children.[13]

The average age for an American woman's first marriage
dropped and the birth rate rose. Proportionally fewer educated women went on to have professional careers than in
the 1930s. A persistent modern stereotype of the American family was born: employed husband with educated
yet career-less wife who looks after several children in the
suburban home. Of course, it has been pointed out that

this image applies only to a certain economic sector of American families at a certain time in history. Yet it remains strong as a stereotype of the typical American family and perhaps as an ideal.

Beatrice Russell's charming story of her life as a Foreign Service wife, *Living in State*, published in 1959, typifies perfectly the general conception of the 1940s and 1950s "good wife," and the ideal, traditional Foreign Service wife. The author's husband entered the Foreign Service in 1949, and their postings in Ethiopia, Tunisia, and Lebanon are described in her book. Russell describes how she reacted to her future husband's goal of becoming a Foreign Service officer:

> In short, the long-cherished picture of myself driving my young executive vice-president to the suburban train in a station wagon was suddenly replaced by a far more glamorous image of myself in the bow of a ship, leaning on the arm of my handsome third secretary as we both gazed eagerly at the distant horizon.[14]

In describing how she, as well as her husband, were briefed in protocol, the behaviors appropriate for one's status in the diplomatic hierarchy, Russell shows that the government took an interest in wives and their behavior. For example, before departing for Ethiopia, Russell learned that in matters of precedence, wives are given the same rank as their husbands: "When entering a car from the left, the ranking wife goes first; but when entering from the right, the junior wife goes first and sits on the far left, thus leaving the right-hand corner for the ranking lady."[15] Such rules were taken seriously at the time; higher-ranking wives could be quite insulted if they were not accorded their proper place or the proper deference.

Russell explains how, before heading off for their first assignment, wives were "invited to attend a lecture on protocol sponsored by the State Department. The primary rule stressed by the lecturer was that wives must call on the chief's wife within the first few days after arriving at a new post."[16] Because Russell was ill upon arrival in Addis

Ababa, she broke rule number one, "but luckily for me, our ambassador's wife was kind and considerate, and showed none of the petty tyranny so often—and for the most part unfairly—attributed to the wives of ranking officers."[17] Here Russell refers to the much-discussed problem of ambassadors' wives tyrannizing the wives of younger officers.

Before 1972, it was officially acceptable for an ambassador's wife to make demands of the other wives, for example requiring their presence and their assistance at social and charitable functions. The term "dragon ladies" has been used to refer to ambassadors' wives who are particularly demanding. While some say their prevalence has been exaggerated, in the interviews conducted for this book I heard many tales of dragon ladies, mostly from the older wives but some even from the younger ones. Russell did eventually make her required calls on the wives of the other diplomats at this post; failure to do so would have been seen as a breach of courtesy.

Russell also tells of a senior officer's wife who invited a subordinate officer's wife to tea for the sole purpose of pointing out that the blouse and skirt she had worn to an embassy cocktail party was inappropriate, saying that "I prefer to see 'my girls' dressed in quiet little silk suits with hats, bags, and gloves."[18] Stories like these, from the pre-1972 days of the Foreign Service, are quite common. The ambassador to Ethiopia at this time, according to Russell, "authored a now-famous protocol memo requesting that embassy ladies not leave their homes without adequate foundation garments."[19]

Russell also explains the importance of diplomatic social activity: "More information can be collected across the dinner table than across a desk, and more useful contacts are developed in the drawing room than in the office."[20] While at some posts (such as larger posts) the junior officers are relatively free from social responsibilities, at other posts all officers and their wives may be called on to do a great deal of socializing. One result is that, as Russell points out, one has to spend a great deal of money for dress clothes. Besides attending countless dinner and cocktail parties, Russell was once told to make five hundred ham sandwiches for the Fourth of July party (which she did, with the help of other wives).

Sociologist Arlie Hochschild's 1969 article "The Role of the Ambassador's Wife: An Exploratory Study" also sheds light on the situation of Foreign Service wives in this era. In 1963, Hochschild observed an ambassador and his wife at post for six months and conducted a mail survey of wives of chiefs of mission. She writes that the role of the ambassador's wife may be termed a "vicarious role" because it is "a role by virtue of one's association with another person's role."[21] The ambassador's wife's role is directly dependent on her husband's role, and while it is not technically a job, it does constitute a full-time role. This is because the role of the diplomat is the extreme version of a representative role, concerned with the relations between the United States and other governments and the people represented by those governments. Because of this representative role, the Foreign Service husband's work carries over more to the spouse than in other occupations, and likewise her behavior reflects upon him.

The role of the wife of the ambassador encompasses as many responsibilities as that of the ambassador himself, although they are of a different nature. As Russell notes, the ambassador's wife is

> expected to be chairman of endless organizations and to sponsor innumerable benefits and charity bazaars.... She must keep a motherly eye on the wives of her husband's subordinate officers. Sick wives must be visited regularly and cheered with books, flowers, and bowls of homemade broth. Unhappy or discontented new wives must somehow be diverted, and new arrivals must be welcomed and introduced to the community. Moreover, if the chief's wife is to be successful in preserving harmony within the official family, she must accomplish all this without offending the sensibilities of the junior wives, who are quick to resent being bossed or patronized.[22]

As head of a hierarchy of embassy wives, then, the wife of the ambassador "must" do all these things; she must watch over "her" wives and uphold the status hierarchy among them while trying to be diplomatic about doing so (lest she be labeled a dragon lady). This hierarchy among the wives is, as already pointed out, defined by the ranks of their husbands. According to Hochschild, "entertaining appropriate people is the chief business of the ambassador's wife, and dinner parties, cocktail parties, luncheons, and teas provide a continual forum in which those in vicarious roles do not 'talk politics' though their presence or absence at such functions is diplomatically 'significant.'"[23] Whom the ambassador's wife does or does not invite, and who does or does not attend, may be seen as politically significant, even if not intended that way.

Despite the great deal of socializing, Hochschild believes that the probability of an ambassador's wife actually making and maintaining deep friendships within these circles is very low. This is due to social barriers and the sheer number of people she must meet and entertain. Much of this socializing is carried out at "the residence," the ambassador's government-owned official home, which is, as Hochschild succinctly describes it, "a large house which looks and feels like a public building and [is] literally owned...by the role rather than the occupant."[24] These residences are completely furnished, so that they may not reflect the occupants' tastes or choices.

One item missing in Russell's account that is present in Hochschild's is a discussion of American women's clubs abroad. Women's clubs serve both a social and a business purpose, as places where wives can, for example, plan and coordinate charitable and community activities. All embassy wives automatically belong. During the period in which Hochschild wrote, the clubs also provided formal ways for senior wives to observe and supervise their subordinates, because the ambassador's wife served (and usually still serves) automatically either as the chairperson or the honorary chairperson.

Hochschild points out that training for a diplomat's wife has increased as her role has come to be seen as more important:

> Accordingly, the Foreign Service Institute now offers briefing sessions for wives, including lectures on American culture and history and foreign policy, guided tours to art museums, and

> language courses.... In addition, a general bib-
> liography is given to all ambassadors' wives....
> The bibliography includes a book on American
> etiquette by Emily Post and two books on dip-
> lomatic etiquette.... [25]

It is likely that the Foreign Service wives of this time, when American women were not encouraged to achieve independently in the outside world, embraced this training and this role because through it they were accorded vicarious status and even a vicarious identity. Rejecting it would not only have brought the group's disapproval, but could have jeopardized the husband's career.

As these authors show, and as will be detailed further by my own interviews, U.S. diplomats' wives have performed countless hours of unpaid work of various types. This work has been an important component of the practice of diplomacy abroad and has contributed to the comfort of Americans at overseas posts. Entertainment and charitable and social activities formed the basis of the role of the American diplomat's wife during this era. Wives had the typical duties pertaining to their own homes, as well as duties relating to the overseas American community and to entertaining. These kinds of activities, traditionally viewed as "woman's work," were deemed necessary to the functioning of the Foreign Service at posts abroad, and wives were evaluated on their ability to perform them. The wives of this era were encouraged to view themselves as part of the team—as adjuncts to their husbands' careers—so that they would serve the U.S. government without compensation. Thus was the role of the Foreign Service wife institutionalized.

The Contemporary American Women's Movement

SINCE THE 1950s and 1960s, women's roles in the Foreign Service have changed substantially, guided by changes occurring in the larger society. By the mid-1960s feminists were attacking the notion that woman's proper place was in the home. In the past quarter-century our society has gone through what is now called the Second Wave of feminism.

Many factors contributed to the growth of the women's movement for equality in the late 1960s. One was the change in women's employment status. During World War II, almost 7 million women were employed for the first time. When the war was over, many of them were demoted or fired, but the postwar economy needed labor, eventually drawing more older and married women into the labor force than ever before. This was significant because prior to the 1960s, most women workers were young and single, and they left paid employment upon marriage. In addition, technical advances in contraception contributed to lower birth rates, and women's life expectancy increased. Women's level of education was also rising. All of these factors clashed with the prevailing ideology of the 1950s that said women could work, but could find true fulfillment only in motherhood and homemaking. White, middle-class, college-educated women saw themselves performing as well as men, but saw also that their status remained lower than that of men. Legal, social, and economic policies worked to reinforce traditional roles and the result was role conflict, or as Friedan dubbed it in *The Feminine Mystique*, the "problem that has no name."

In the political arena, women's issues were recognized as having some importance by 1961, when President Kennedy established a Presidential Commission on the Status of Women. The commission's report detailing evidence of gender inequality was released in 1965. Fifty state commissions were established to carry out similar research on the state level. The existence of these commissions created the expectation that something would be done to ameliorate women's status in society. Title VII of the 1964 Civil Rights Act banned sex, as well as race, discrimination in employment. However, the article which referred to women was tacked onto the bill as a ploy by Representative Howard Smith of Virginia (he believed that adding sex to the bill would guarantee that it would not pass) and was initially not enforced by the Equal Employment Opportunity Commission. Partly out of rage over this situation, and facilitated by the growing networks of educated and professional middle-class women, Friedan and others formed the National Organization for Women

in 1966 to "take action to bring women into full participation in the mainstream of American society."[26]

One result of the women's movement was a transformation in the marital relationship between middle-class
husbands and wives. As record numbers of women left
the home to pursue careers of their own, a parallel shift in
their relationship to their husbands occurred: fewer women
were defining themselves as housewife and husband's
helper. Indeed, for many the word "housewife," representing what was once an honorable role for a woman,
took on a derogatory tone.

The Women's Movement Within the Foreign Service

THE FOREIGN SERVICE wives of the pre-women's movement era were much like other middle- and upper-class
wives of America, with several additional factors at work.
Following one's husband meant following him anywhere
in the world, often far from family and friends. And because the Foreign Service life abroad requires representational work, wives at overseas posts had their time filled
with the planning and carrying out of social and community events. Such activities seemed to fall "naturally" to
the women, and for some time this work was obligatory.
It was widely accepted that with the hiring of an employee,
the Department of State got a "two-fer"—two-for-the-
price-of-one—the paid employee and his unpaid wife.

In the early 1970s, in step with other American
women, some Foreign Service wives rebelled and began
to voice dissatisfaction with the requirements placed on
them by the Foreign Service. Like wives all over America,
they were performing services for which they were not
reimbursed. Yet, unlike other wives, they could not extri-
cate themselves from the world of their husband's work
and find their own arena of professional fulfillment.

As the wider society began to advocate gender equality, the Foreign Service followed suit in the 1970s. In the
years following passage of the Civil Rights Act, the U.S.
government placed a new emphasis on issues of equal employment opportunity, and these new policies required

research. In the Department of State a management study was undertaken to formulate and implement a "Program for the Seventies" that would institute new equal employment opportunity procedures and regulations. One focus was women officers of the Foreign Service: their recruitment; their role in the Foreign Service; and discrimination against them.

An Ad Hoc Committee to Improve the Status of Women in Foreign Affairs Agencies was formed, and it made five major recommendations: to increase the number of women in the Foreign Service, to abolish all kinds of discrimination, to abolish discrimination against married women in particular, to have women serve on all selection boards and panels, and to consider the role of women in all task force reports. A "Policy on the Assignment of Women and Minority Personnel" (1970) was issued, reiterating the goal of equal employment opportunity. By 1971 new regulations were approved by the Department of State, USIA, and USAID to make marriage and a career in the Foreign Service compatible for women. Wording in recruitment literature was changed to clarify the point that marriage or intention to marry would be no bar to entry into the Foreign Service. All women officers who had previously been required to resign their jobs upon marriage were offered reappointment.

These changes were in part due to the work of the Women's Action Organization (WAO), which was formed in 1970 to represent the women—secretaries, officers, and wives—in the Department of State, USIA, and USAID. This mobilization of women occurred out of a concern that women's problems were not being considered in the management reforms to modernize the Foreign Service in the 1970s. WAO literature described the organization as "no ladies sewing circle" and defined its purpose as "to improve the opportunities for promotions, assignments, training, and perquisites stateside and abroad for all categories of women employees and Foreign Service spouses."[27]

Consideration of women employees was also spurred by the Alison Palmer case, the first major sex discrimination case against the Department of State, which was filed in 1971. Palmer claimed a pattern of discrimination by sex in the overseas assignments given her. For example, upon arrival as a labor officer in Ethiopia, the ambassador there assigned her to be his wife's executive assistant. Palmer won her case, and the Department conceded that discrimination had occurred.

However, the 1971 assurance of career-marriage compatibility was directed for the most part toward the female employee, not the female spouse. The 1971 Department Notice, "Implementing Policy on Equal Opportunities for Women and Employment Abroad of Dependents of Employees," noted that dependents with appropriate qualifications would be eligible for consideration for employment in the foreign affairs agencies and also should be considered for employment in the local economy where possible. Interested dependents were instructed to contact the appropriate head of the overseas establishment, and embassies were instructed to survey families to determine which dependents desired employment. However, no formal system was as yet set up to organize or implement such employment.

The '72 Directive

WITH THE support of the WAO, in 1972 a "Policy on Wives of Foreign Service Employees" was issued that began as follows: "The Department believes that the tradition of husband and wife teams and of wives' participation in the representational activities of a post has been one of the major strengths of the Foreign Service."[28] However, the Department allowed that it must recognize women's changing role in society:

> In the past few years, rapid changes in American society have provided wider roles for women than were traditionally available. Women have gained increasing recognition of their right to be treated as individuals and to have personal and career interests in addition to their more traditional roles as wife or mother. If the Foreign Service is to remain representative of American society, and if its traditions are to be

preserved and strengthened, the Foreign Service must adapt to these changing conditions.[29]

Thus was the Department of State policy changed to reflect the new national goal of equality between the sexes;
Foreign Service wives were proclaimed to be private persons. No longer would they be required to carry out any
duties for the government of the United States.

Six points are covered in the policy. Foremost, the wife
of a Foreign Service employee is declared to be a private
individual and not a government employee; thus the Foreign Service has no right to levy any duties upon her. The
policy states that while representational activities are a large
part of the Foreign Service career, the U.S. government
has no right to insist that the wife of an officer carry out
such responsibilities: "Each wife must decide the extent to
which she wants to participate as a partner in this aspect of
her husband's job."[30] In addition, while charitable activities
on the part of wives are recognized as contributing favorably to the image of the United States abroad, a wife's participation in them would now be voluntary, including her
participation in clubs or any social gatherings.

The fourth point, that no wife is given authority over
the wives of other employees, was included because of a
problem mentioned above: incidents of wives of senior
officers making unnecessary and demeaning demands on
wives of junior officers. The fifth point abolishes the practice of evaluating wives' social participation and representational activities in husbands' performance reports. Last,
the policy states that all regulations will be reviewed to
ensure that they comply with these new guidelines, and
the policy is explicit in that it states that it is applicable to
male spouses and other dependents of Foreign Service
employees as well as to wives.

As for what can be expected or required of the spouse
by the Department of State, the new policy lists only one
item: "It can only require that she comport herself in a
manner which will not reflect discredit on the United
States."[31]

It has been said that this new policy, widely referred
to as the '72 Directive, liberated the Foreign Service wife.

No longer could the Department of State expect "two-for-the-price-of-one." However, while many agree that the '72 Directive was necessary, some believe it has actually created more problems than it has solved, and that if given the choice most wives would have vetoed it. Spouses were not consulted in forming the policy; only one spouse was on the drafting committee. One Foreign Service wife has written that as a consequence of the policy, spouses who "continue to perform voluntarily the traditional duties of diplomacy" are disenfranchised, cast "into a netherworld of nonrecognition,"[32] so that unofficially, "two-for-the-price-of-one" still holds true. Because the role, and expectations of the role, were so entrenched, liberation did not come easily.

Violations of the departmental policy statements on the equality of women and the status of spouses and other dependents as private citizens occasioned a 1975 directive, instructing posts to ensure compliance on a number of points, including the following: (1) spouses cannot be ordered to make social calls or attend coffees; (2) spouses cannot be forced or pressured into joining community action or socially oriented organizations such as Embassy spouse clubs; (3) posts should take note of increasing numbers of male spouses and should attempt to make them comfortable participating in post activities; and (4) female employees cannot be instructed to make a courtesy call which a male employee is not required to make.

Foreign Service Women and Employment

As INCREASING numbers of women in the larger society began to pursue their own careers, the issue of paid employment for Foreign Service spouses began to demand attention. In 1975 a committee of the WAO was created to study the issue. The committee called for urgent attention to be given to several needs, especially employment for spouses. Recommendations included establishing a skills bank where spouses who desire work overseas could register, listing employment and educational opportunities for spouses at overseas posts, negotiating bilateral agreements with other countries for spouse employment in the local economy, and encouraging chiefs of missions to use spouses' talents and training overseas.

In 1976, a group of former and current female Foreign Service officers filed a class action lawsuit, *Palmer* v. *Baker,* which alleged discrimination by the Department of State in the recruiting, testing, and hiring process of the Foreign Service. After ten years, the women won their case. At first it was decided that as the Department had done earlier with minority test-takers, female test-takers would be allowed to pass the written examination with a score lower than that required for white males to pass. Later, the scoring of examinations was adjusted further, so that separate rank order lists of male and female candidates were created, based on their examination scores. An equal number of males and females were then identified as having passed the test. Thus today female candidates who score lower than some male candidates may pass, while some males who score higher than some females may fail.[33] This has led one observer to remark that "women FSOs may now have to face a new prejudice, an assumption that they are less qualified than their male colleagues."[34]

In 1978 the Family Liaison Office (FLO) was created "with the mandate of responding to the needs of Foreign Service families as they try to cope with the disruptions caused by a mobile lifestyle and service abroad."[35] FLO fulfilled the 1975 recommendation from the WAO to establish a skills bank for Foreign Service family members. Spouses may provide information about their education, training, skills, and previous employment, which is maintained in the computerized skills bank and sent in advance to overseas posts, so that spouses may be informed before their move if employment will be available. Through this service spouses may also find placements with other foreign affairs agencies, private voluntary organizations, or international businesses at overseas posts, and may obtain help in locating employment during their Washington, D.C., stays.

FLO also negotiates bilateral work agreements with other nations, which provide that spouses and dependents of U.S. government officials posted abroad may seek work in the local economy. The United States currently has bilateral work agreements with sixty-three countries (some of which restrict the number of family members permitted to work or restrict the type of employment). In addition, agreements have been made with sixty-one other countries to allow spouses and dependents of Foreign Service officers to apply for work permits through special channels.

FLO has expanded its employment services to include individual counseling, a resource library, and courses on job search strategies. Spouses may also enroll, on a space available basis, in Foreign Service Institute courses (for example, consular, administrative, and advanced word processing classes are offered). A Career Development Resource Center offers career planning workshops and career development programs in addition to individual career counseling.

In 1985, Senator Charles McC. Mathias, Jr., a Republican from Maryland, introduced a proposal directing the Secretary of State to develop a plan for the employment of Foreign Service spouses, which won passage. State Department personnel worked to negotiate additional agreements with foreign governments to enable spouses to work in the local economy when abroad. At posts overseas, qualified spouses are matched with vacant jobs. Once a spouse has worked at a post for one year (in certain kinds of positions), she (or he) is eligible for work at the Department of State or any other government agency upon return to the United States (this is called executive order eligibility). Summer employment is also provided at most embassies for teenage and college-age dependents. However, a *New York Times* article quotes a State Department personnel officer who asserts that the real challenge is to provide meaningful employment, rather than support work, for spouses.[36]

A recent development on the employment front has been the Rockefeller Amendment. This legislation allows non-Foreign Service-affiliated Americans abroad to apply for positions that previously were reserved for Foreign Service family members. While Foreign Service family members have priority among qualified candidates, they must now face competition for employment opportunities abroad with American corporate spouses.

U.S. Department of State officials have thus attempted to adjust to changing times by attending to the criticisms and desires of Foreign Service spouses. Wives are no longer officially regarded as extensions of their husbands, and their time and energy are no longer at the disposal of the Department of State. Yet Foreign Service officers must still accept posts worldwide, and our economy is not so global as to make employment available for American spouses everywhere. Some wives continue to lament that they are expected to perform representational and community service duties; dinner parties still must be given and receptions still must be attended. Many still feel pressure to become active in embassy wives' associations.

It is clear from the many hours I have spent interviewing Foreign Service wives that the change in official policy went only so far in quelling dissatisfaction. First, no single statement could possibly have transformed entire structures that had existed for decades. Second, the need for the unpaid work women do remains. Not only did the policy statement not ameliorate the wives' plight, but it created a wide gulf between women who value and embrace the traditional role and those who want no part of it—each group is seen as disparaging the other's choice. And even with the policy, spouses who desire careers of their own while remaining married to a Foreign Service officer still face logistical difficulties.

Spouses Speak for Themselves: The Report on the Role of the Spouse in the Foreign Service

IN THE early 1980s, the Association of American Foreign Service Women (an independent, voluntary group) sponsored a study on the role of the spouse in the Foreign Service. Over 10,000 questionnaires were mailed to spouses of employees of the different foreign affairs agencies. The authors state that every agency, area of the world, age group, type and size of post, rank of employee, and number of children is represented in the final sample of 4,200 spouses, or 40 percent of the targeted population.

Male spouses were included, but the vast majority of spouses who responded were female.

While many of those surveyed said that they enjoy Foreign Service life in general, the results point to the existence of two camps of Foreign Service spouses. The majority of the respondents said they find the representational role time-consuming, boring, and personally not very fulfilling, but a sizable proportion said that engaging in representational activities gives them a feeling of purpose overseas. Over two-thirds of the spouses feel that they have no real free choice in this matter, because the representational role is still fully expected of them. Those who do perform such duties said they do so to help their partners, rather than to aid the goals of the government, and the vast majority said their partners show appreciation for this. Over half would like official recognition at post; these spouses said that if their role at post were official they would be more committed to the Foreign Service. However, the rest want no official recognition. Thus, Foreign Service spouses appear to be divided between those who reject the representational role and those who desire it, albeit in a more recognized and rewarded way.

The responses to the survey reveal a drop in commitment to the Foreign Service over the past decade; the sense of idealism and pride found in Beatrice Russell's description of her life in the Foreign Service has diminished. The spouses with the highest morale are those who are *not* part of a two-person career but have paying jobs or portable careers and are not overburdened with representational duties. The spouses of senior Foreign Service officers, who perform three times the amount of representational work as nonsenior spouses, had the lowest morale. In general, senior wives said they are dissatisfied, not with their role and the Foreign Service lifestyle, but with their ambiguous status. They are discontented with being neither official public persons nor private citizens. They perceive that the contributions of which they are proud are considered nonessential by others, leading to feelings of having wasted years of their lives doing unpaid, unrecognized work. Thus about two-thirds of the wives of senior officers said that their commitment to the Foreign

Service would increase if their contributions were officially recognized. Interestingly, the majority of the sample as a whole agreed that the ambassador's wife should provide a leadership role, indicating that the Foreign Service community continues to look toward senior spouses as having a special status and responsibilities.

The foremost concern of the spouses surveyed was for improved employment opportunities overseas. The Foreign Service lifestyle limits career choice and inhibits career development of spouses, but economic need prescribes a two-income family, and high rates of divorce make self-sufficiency important. In addition, Foreign Service spouses are no different from other Americans in viewing pay as a measure of worth; almost two-thirds of the respondents said that a paying job is vital to their self-esteem. Three-quarters of the spouses surveyed said that they wish to work, and most of these stated that they want not just any job, but meaningful work. Yet only slightly over half of the spouses surveyed were employed at the time of the study, and two-fifths of the working spouses stated that their jobs were not career-oriented.

Regarding the '72 Directive, the authors of the study state:

> We believe that the so-called progressive attitudes concerning the traditional Foreign Service partnership were, in essence, a giant put-down of those spouses who needed no broader purpose in life than to be a wife and mother in the Foreign Service.[37]

The authors argue that the '72 Directive that was supposed to set spouses "free" only served to devalue the work they had done and proclaim their good labors no longer necessary. It is evident from this research that while the work of the spouse continues, a gap exists between official policy towards spouses and the reality of their lives. The gulf between the "traditional" and the "modern" spouses that I described earlier is also apparent. Clearly, there is still a problem.

Conclusion

OFFICIAL POLICY toward Foreign Service spouses has changed dramatically. Wives were once expected to perform representational duties and indeed, they were rated on their ability to do so. The husband-wife team was considered by the Department to be a "two-fer"—two employees for the price of one. While Foreign Service spouses have not yet acquired the right to financial compensation for their representational labor, they are now officially recognized as private persons and no longer as working extensions of their husbands.

However, as I will show in the following chapters, wives' feelings about these changes very greatly, depending on when they grew up and the choices available to them. For those who entered adulthood before women were commonly allowed to achieve professionally for themselves, being adjuncts to their diplomat husbands brought them opportunities and adventure which they were unlikely to experience otherwise. The attitudes of these "traditional" wives toward the Foreign Service are presented and discussed in the next chapter. In the following two chapters, we hear from the younger generation. Their perspectives on their status as Foreign Service wives are certainly much different from those of the older wives. While the latter stress their commitment to their husbands and their husbands' employer, the former question their commitment to each.

NOTES

1. Lord Gore-Booth, ed., *Satow's Guide to Diplomatic Practice*, 5th ed. (London and New York: Longman, 1979), pp. 162–3.

2. W. Wendell Blancké, *The Foreign Service of the United States* (New York: Praeger, 1969), p. 12.

3. Martin Weil, *A Pretty Good Club: The Founding Fathers of the United States Foreign Service* (New York: W.W. Norton, 1978), p. 15.

4. Blancké, *The Foreign Service of the United States*, p. 19.

5. Weil, *A Pretty Good Club*, p. 47.

6. Ibid., p. 20.

7. Ibid., p. 47.

8. William J. Lederer and Eugene Burdick, *The Ugly American* (New York: Fawcett Crest, 1958), p. 230.

9. Ibid., p. 237.

10. Homer L. Calkin, *Women in the Department of State: Their Role in American Foreign Affairs* (Washington, DC: U.S. Department of State, 1978).

11. As quoted in Jewell Fenzi, *Married to the Foreign Service: An Oral History of the American Diplomatic Spouse* (New York: Twayne, 1994), p. 131.

12. Blancké, *The Foreign Service of the United States*, p. 84.

13. Betty Friedan, *The Feminine Mystique* (New York: Laurel, 1983 ed., originally published in 1963), p. 15–16.

14. Beatrice Russell, *Living in State* (New York: David McKay, 1959) p. 4.

15. Ibid., p. 53.

16. Ibid., p. 45.

17. Ibid

18. Ibid., p. 55.

19. Ibid., pp. 55–56.

20. Ibid., p. 83.

21. Arlie Hochschild, "The Role of the Ambassador's Wife: An Exploratory Study," *Journal of Marriage and the Family* 31, 1 (February 1969), p. 73.

22. Russell, *Living in State*, pp. 84–5.

23. Hochschild, "The Role of the Ambassador's Wife," p. 80.

24. Ibid., p. 84.

25. Ibid., p. 76.

26. Friedan, *The Feminine Mystique*, p. 384.

27. Calkin, *Women in the Department of State*, p. 253.

28. As reproduced in Calkin, *Women in the Department of State,* p. 278.

29. Calkin, *Women in the Department of State*, p. 279.

30. Ibid.

31. Ibid.

32. Jewell Fenzi, "The Great Divorce: Why the 'Hands-Off' Policy Did More Harm than Good for Spouses," *Foreign Service Journal* (June 1992), pp. 18, 21.

33. Typically, 12,000–13,000 people take the yearly Foreign Service examination. Those who pass the written examination, generally a pool of 2,500 candidates, must still pass an oral assessment, where women have tended to do as well as men. Usually, approximately 200 new junior officers enter each year. The 1995 examination was canceled because of lack of need for new junior officers.

34. James Workman, "Gender Norming," *New Republic* (July 1, 1991), p. 16.

35. Family Liaison Office, *Family Liaison Office: Overview* (Washington, DC: U.S. Department of State, May 1990).

36. *New York Times,* "State Department: To Pay or Not to Pay the Spouse" (November 2, 1985), sect. 1, p. 7.

37. The Role of the Spouse Committee of the Forum, *Report on the Role of the Spouse in the Foreign Service: A Study of Attitudes and Perceptions of Spouses Toward Foreign Service Life* (Washington, DC: U.S. Department of State: 1985), p. 45.

4

The Traditional Wives: Committed to Husband and Country

MUCH OF THIS CHAPTER is based on personal interviews with twenty-one women who represent the older generation of Foreign Service wives. Their average age was 58 at the time that they were interviewed, with most having become adults in the 1950s. Most entered the Foreign Service in the 1960s, when their husband entered or they married a Foreign Service officer. They have on average two children, but some have up to five. Two wives are foreign-born; both are originally from European countries.

The depiction of the American family of the 1950s—working husband, stay-at-home mom, two or more children—remains firmly implanted in our culture as the ideal American family, which represented the best of America during the best of times. In keeping with this ideal, the majority of the traditional women came from middle-class homes where their mothers did not work for pay. Catherine, fifty-six years old with three children, told me,

> I've talked about this with friends of our age. We started school just after the war. And in the social milieu that I grew up in, when you said, well, her mother worked, well that told you a whole bunch of things. I mean, her mother *works*. Most of the people that I grew up with, their mothers did not work. And it wasn't what you aspired to. If her mother had to work, well then, she wasn't at home, she *had* to work. Or

they weren't rich enough, she had to work. So
that meant they weren't middle-class or they
were lower-middle-class. Or, she was divorced.
Those were the values you grow up with. You're
a housewife...you don't work. The men did the
work.

These comments demonstrate the ideal of the time, that
a wife shouldn't "have" to work. Only one wife described
her childhood family as being "poor"; when her parents
were separated, her mother took a job as a child-care
worker in order to support the family. None of the other
women's parents were divorced or separated during their
formative years.

This was also the time when *The Ugly American*, with
its portrayal of American diplomats as bumbling incom-
petents, was published. In my conversations with these
women, two of them mentioned the book; one stated that
she had read it before she met her Foreign Service officer
husband and therefore initially was unreceptive to him,
while the other said,

In those days, there were people who were very
suspicious of American diplomats. Americans
themselves were very suspicious of the State
Department. This was after the McCarthy era,
and there had been a book written called *The
Ugly American* and if you said you were in the
State Department they looked at you, wonder-
ing if you were one of *those*. (Emma)

Emma and others felt the repercussions of this book. These
wives' husbands entered the Foreign Service at a time when
the diplomatic corps was suffering an image crisis.

"It Fit In with the Way I Had Been Brought Up"

WHILE ALL of the older wives I interviewed had some un-
pleasant memories, overall these women felt that the Foreign Service experience was a positive one, and most
frequently I heard the word "adventure" in describing their
Foreign Service years. In spite of the fact that most of

them served at a time when wives were most taken advantage of, the women I spoke with had no animosity toward the Foreign Service.

The reason for this is that most wives of this generation had no career plans for themselves. All but one have at least a bachelor's degree, so this is a well-educated group. Yet in keeping with the expectations of the era, fewer than half thought in terms of a specific career for themselves:

> I was definitely Midwest, definitely a product of the Eisenhower years, and as much as I pooh-poohed it, we were all going to university and basically hoping to meet somebody.... So no, I can't say that I was encouraged to go out and take on the world. (Catherine)

Of those who said they had something in mind other than marriage or children, teaching or academic careers were mentioned as possibilities, and several said they were interested in travel and/or languages. A few of those who had prepared for a particular profession told me that they had done so not because they were interested in pursuing a career but because their parents, who had lived through the Depression, had stressed the necessity of being able to support themselves. Ruth, with a degree in English, said,

> I did end up getting a teaching credential.... But it was pretty much I think what women did in those years. There were a limited range of options that you perceived, it's not that the options weren't there. And of course I got married and went overseas.... So I really didn't see myself on a career track or with some long-range goal.

I asked if she had ever thought about having to support herself someday:

> It's a wonderful question. And yes, my father in particular had that as a very high goal for me, because he, like my mother, of course they'd come through the Depression, and really did

think in those terms. But teaching.... It was stable. And whether I wanted to do that or not was irrelevant. And also whether I was suited for it. And I never saw myself really as a teacher.

Those who did seek a profession, whether because of economic necessity or for their own fulfillment, tended to pursue careers that were traditionally thought of as "women's work," such as education, office work, and airline hostessing. As Gail, who holds a master's degree in teaching, described the situation:

When I finished college, women seemed to have choices of being teachers or nurses or going to Catherine Gibbs and getting into publishing after they became secretaries.

These women, then, experienced no clash between their husband's, or future husband's, plans for the Foreign Service and any plans of their own. For most, getting married and having children were their primary goals:

I'm not committed to career in the way that a lot of people are, a lot of women are, and that's fine. It's just that, I'm always perfectly happy to work, but I didn't feel any need, any personal need, to have a career that went from year to year. (Betty)

Indeed, many of these wives told me that the Foreign Service was attractive to them because it was an opportunity to do something out of the ordinary. They especially liked the idea of travel. Betty and Vivian were two of several women who expressed a love for travel:

I thought it was exciting, I thought it was going to be fun to travel and do those kinds of things.

Aside from being in love with my husband, what lured me was the opportunity to travel.

However, besides knowing that a Foreign Service career meant travel, few wives knew much else about the job or the lifestyle. "I had no idea what it was," Arlene said.

Some of these wives did not think much—or at all—about the effects of their husband's career on their own lives: "I was in love and I wanted to get married and it fit in with the way I had been brought up," said Sophie. Another said, "I didn't give it a great deal of thought. I figured we'd be together wherever we were and it would be okay" (Elaine). When I asked Jean, who came of age during World War II, how she felt about the prospect of moving around with her husband's job, she told me,

> This was a very turbulent period for a young girl to grow up. Most of us had had either date rape or something similar to it, because of the war circumstance. If we married the person, then we were lucky, but if we didn't, we'd already had a number of experiences, some of them quite unpleasant. And to find a good man, a nice man, a fine man, was just very important to us.... And I think my whole life was determined by finding a man from a family I understood, a man I understood.... And I think the character of the man changed my life, more than the business of traveling around.

Clearly, Jean would have married this man no matter what his chosen career; to her, his being a Foreign Service officer was neither a plus nor a minus. She married the man, and then happily became part of his career. We will see that this attitude is much less common with the younger generation of Foreign Service wives.

Other wives exhibited total acquiescence in their husbands' career decisions. Emma's husband began in the State Department as a Civil Service officer who worked in the area of foreign affairs but was not assigned abroad. When asked how she felt about her husband's later transferring to the Foreign Service, Emma said, "Well, it was the thing to do, there was no question about his not doing it, being in the State Department. That was the way things happened." To this day she does not perceive her right to have feelings about it one way or the other. Edith, who eventually earned a doctorate, had difficult experiences at her husband's first post in the early 1960s but said, "There was a commitment in that time. I had made a commitment to my husband, and that was what he was doing, and I survived, I guess." For these wives, commitment to their husband meant adapting themselves to his life and career.

Besides the excitement and glamour of travel and their unquestioned commitment to their husband and his career, the women noted one other motivating factor: patriotic duty. In spite of the negative perceptions of the Foreign Service that resulted from *The Ugly American*, serving one's country was very important to many of these wives. Margaret eloquently expresses this attitude:

> I always felt that it would be very important to serve your country. Service is something that is really integral...service to community and church and school, and that was a real important part of my upbringing as it was my husband's.

Thus, the Foreign Service wives of the older generation derived their role from their commitment to their husbands and to their country. For these women, the decision to tie themselves to the Foreign Service was not something that they agonized over. Indeed, for some it was an exciting, unique opportunity, given the choices they had. They did not view being a Foreign Service wife as a tradeoff for a career and/or an identity of their own.

The Official Word: Wives Will Support Their Husbands

THAT THE wife of the Foreign Service officer had a particular role and special duties was made very clear to the women themselves in the years before the '72 Directive,

during orientation sessions and classes for wives held at
the Foreign Service Institute. Wives who had attended
these classes said that their role was described in terms of
patriotic duty; they were made to feel an important part
of a "team." Sophie said,

> We were told that we were wives, and we were
> to help our husbands, and we were very fortu-
> nate to be able to go off and be in this elite
> group of people, the cream of the crop I think
> we were told we were, to go off and help our
> husbands serve our country. And the idea of
> serving my country had a great deal of appeal
> for me.

Sophie and her fiancé were both accepted into the Foreign Service at about the same time, but she was told that
she could not sign on if she was to be married. In contrast
to men, who were looked upon more favorably if they
were married, women were accepted into the pre-1972
Foreign Service only if they were single, and they had to
resign if they later married. Sophie decided to become a
Foreign Service wife instead of a Foreign Service officer:

> I still felt like I was going to serve my country.
> So this idea of two-for-the-price-of-one didn't
> bother me in those days. You know, I still
> thought I was going to go and do it, that I had
> an important role to play. So all of that didn't
> rub the wrong way on me in those days.

Thus wives were told, and felt themselves, that they
could make a contribution through their own sphere of
influence in the special role of the Foreign Service officer's
wife. In the late 1950s, Louise attended an orientation
session:

> I remember asking a question, saying I was a
> secondary school teacher, do you think that in
> the Foreign Service there would be opportuni-
> ties to use my profession, and this person said,

> you are in the Foreign Service to support your
> husband in his endeavors.

Wives were encouraged to put aside any thoughts of fulfillment from other directions.

Some wives were unable to attend sessions at the Foreign Service Institute because they were caring for children
or were not in the Washington, D.C., area for any length of
time. Today, limited funding is available for child care; then,
there were no such funds. A few of the traditional wives said
they were not even aware that such classes existed, either
because the State Department neglected to publicize them
or because their husbands did not bother to suggest them.

Once at post, official personnel instructed wives about
appropriate behavior. Claire, a very independent woman
who has made a career for herself in the Civil Service over
the years, has never forgotten being admonished by the
consul general himself. He complained that instead of help-
ing to serve coffee at a party in his home, she had talked at
length to the guest of honor. But some wives were very
happy to pitch in immediately at post by doing such things
as making food for large receptions, feeling that this was
how they could do "their part":

> You know, I'm just that kind of person. I've al-
> ways given, and you wouldn't even have to ask
> me. I did it gladly, I wanted to do it, I wanted
> to be a part of it.... And I feel a certain amount
> of alienation toward the new Foreign Service
> because people don't do it, they won't do it.
> And I think to myself, marriages are a union,
> you really do work together, and anyone who
> goes into the Foreign Service, if they don't un-
> derstand it, then they're headed for trouble.
> They're really headed for trouble if they don't
> understand this is a commitment. (Margaret)

For Margaret, as for others, the husband's commitment
to the Foreign Service meant that the wife had the same
commitment. The women of this generation see the Foreign Service as a two-person career.

Tales of Dragon Ladies

BEFORE THE '72 Directive, hierarchies of wives existed at post. As in the military, not only were there rankings of officers, but also of their wives.[1] Wives of senior officers at post were called "senior wives" (and often still are). Senior wives who saw overseeing junior wives as part of their role have been called "dragon ladies." As Beatrice Russell described in *Living in State*, in the old days new wives were required to make calls on wives already at post, along with other duties. "Dragon ladies" felt that it was their job to watch over new wives and to make sure they were behaving appropriately. Younger wives cooperated because they knew their behavior was being officially evaluated and that the wife of the superior officer had some part in this evaluation, since it was her husband who was writing the report.

Several tales of "dragon ladies" emerged in my interviews with the older generation. Greta, a German-born wife, told of her experiences at her husband's first post in 1962:

> They were quite tyrannical actually. The woman had her niche there as being the wife of the consul and it was actually a large consulate. So she had probably twenty wives, and she really ruled with an iron fist, she checked up on you to see if you made your calls. And she had monthly teas and you'd better show up. And I think this was typical, that we had to leave our kids with a strange somebody, somebody's maid. We were monitored, we were watched, and we were told if we hadn't made our calls on time, or if we hadn't made all our calls.

I asked Greta if she knew she was going to be written up on her husband's efficiency report, and she replied,

> Yes. We knew that. Our husbands knew it, so our husbands would go along with it and say, "Do the best you can, dear" (laughs). And one day she even announced in one of her teas, that "Well, you know, my husband is writing your

husband's efficiency reports these days, and you
know there is this part about the wife, so it's
very stressed and so you'd better...."

It was certainly made clear to Greta that her behavior would
reflect upon her husband and his evaluation as an employee.

Yet Renate, another foreign-born wife, described the
positive aspects of demands such as making calls:

> You very quickly got to know people, you have
> seen their house, you have seen them in their
> house. And you exchanged information, and you
> knew who was who. And after that when you
> met them at a reception or something, you knew
> who it was.

Gail remembers being required to attend classes in
manners held by the wife of the senior political/economic
officer in India in the late 1960s. And Kay, whose first
tour was in the early 1970s, tells the following story:

> My husband had arrived at post before I, and he
> had gotten to know his boss's wife, and I think
> he immediately knew there was going to be
> trouble, because she was a very bossy type, and
> had already planned out everything I was going
> to do for her when I got there. I didn't know
> what I had in store for me when I arrived with
> my brand-new baby, that within forty-eight hours
> she had a long list of things that she expected me
> to do within the next week. Call on all the offi-
> cers' wives, serve tea, serve cookies, bake cook-
> ies. She had a long list of things that were required
> of me when I first arrived. And I was totally taken
> aback and I basically said I was sorry but I could
> not. And that was the first time anybody had said
> no to her. And I remember there being a big
> issue in the embassy, because I was the first wife
> that had really said no. Oh, it became a big, big
> issue. I remember being at a party and this woman
> coming up to me and my husband and saying,

> "You know, it's too bad, your husband has a lot
> of potential but he'll never make it as an ambas-
> sador with you as his wife."[2]

Just after this incident, the '72 Directive was issued, resolv-
ing the immediate problem for Kay and her husband. Yet it
is evident that wives were pressured to conform; they were
pressed into service and viewed as extensions of their husbands. It is especially interesting that while this two-person
career system was implicit, if not official Department of State
policy, the system was perpetuated by wives themselves. If
the only way for these women to have status was to derive it
from their husbands, some were certainly going to use the
status, once acquired, and demand the deference they felt
they deserved as a "senior wife."

Wives' Clubs

As DESCRIBED earlier, women's or wives' clubs have served
to define and maintain status for Foreign Service wives, as
well as being places to exchange information and socialize. The vast majority of the wives in this chapter participated in women's group activities, and several women said
they were pressured into doing so. Gail, who experienced
"strong pressure" to join the women's club at one post,
described it as "something to occupy women" who had
nothing better to do. In contrast, Sophie, who had for-
saken her own career as a Foreign Service officer, saw a
benefit in being forced to participate:

> Somebody actually called me up and told me I
> had to participate in the American Women's
> Club. And I remember feeling sort of resentful
> about that, because the baby was pretty little,
> and I wasn't quite ready to go out and socialize.
> In retrospect it was a great thing, because it got
> me out of the house, and it turned out that the
> women were just delightful and it was probably
> the most interesting thing that I did.

Thus, these clubs sometimes acted as a built-in social structure and support system. Women's or wives' clubs, also

found in the military, could be useful as sources of practical information or as places to make friends.

Volunteer activities were often planned within these clubs. Volunteer work often carries enhanced status, a strong motivator. In addition, given the era and the circumstances, there often wasn't much else for the women to do. Alice said that charitable activities "are not especially my bag but that's what there was to do." Yet the volunteerism of Foreign Service wives is unique, because in many cases it was motivated by the women's genuine shock at the appalling conditions in some countries. Foreign Service wives have had a hand in such worthwhile projects as running an orphanage in an African country, raising funds to install running water at a maternity hospital, aiding refugees, organizing international schools where there had been none before, and many more.

"Dreary, Dangerous, Unhealthy" Yet "Tremendously Fun": Foreign Posts

THE TRADITIONAL wives served in different parts of the world with their husbands. Expectations about wives' role and duties were determined by the particular characteristics of a post and the rank of the husband. For example, in larger posts, wives of junior officers may not have had to entertain very much, while senior wives may have been very busy with representational work. In very small posts, there may be a great deal of pressure for everyone to "pitch in" with entertainment.

One might think that living in a less-developed country, where conditions are relatively difficult, may cause a wife to view the Foreign Service experience negatively, but for these older wives this is not the case. When one enters the Foreign Service, one knows that at some point, probably sooner rather than later, there will be an assignment to a "hardship" post—that comes with the promise of "worldwide availability" that a Foreign Service officer makes. These wives looked back on their hardship posts with pride in their accomplishments in those places. Said Jean, whose husband served in many important positions in the Middle East in the 1950s and 1960s,

It was a time when everything you did was the
first time, because there hadn't been very many
things done. Do you know what I mean? There
just hadn't been that many people in those particular Middle Eastern posts. And so we sort of
set things up, a number of things.

Instead of having the attitude that there was less to do in
such places than in, say, Paris, these women saw how they
could actually be more useful in a hardship post. In addition to being helpful to the host country nationals through
such volunteer projects as were described earlier, wives
also saw that they could be of assistance to the other Americans there:

I think I just had an instinct that I could help
people out. The place where we were all having
a terrible time was in the Philippines. Everybody
was having a terrible time, so I figured I would
do to the best of my ability what I thought
needed to be done to help us as a community
to get through this very difficult time. (Arlene)

Repeatedly, the women commented that while life
was hard at times, it wasn't the Foreign Service as a whole
that made it so. Martha, a New Englander who was sent
with her husband to a Middle Eastern country in the late
1960s, had no washing machine, no hot running water,
and no air conditioning. Yet she says that, looking back,

I don't resent the Foreign Service now. I resented it in ——, but it wasn't the Service. It
was where you were, and the insensitivity of certain administrative officers and the inability to
get certain comforts that I thought we needed,
like an air conditioner.

Foreign Service wives know that each assignment will last
only two to three years, so if they are at a post they don't
particularly like, they can bear it; the next place will probably be better. Some remarked, too, that what was most

important at a post was not what the town or city or country itself had to offer—or lacked—it was what the people had to offer in the way of friendships. Margaret, whose first post was an African country in the 1970s, said that

> The first post was tremendously fun.... It was awful in so many respects, but there were so many interesting people. It was multinational. So there were just fascinating people. So while life was dreary, dangerous, unhealthy, expensive, nothing to do, very little culture available, there were so many interesting people. So there was an incredible exchange of ideas and culture.

Overall, then, the effects of the type of post on a wife's satisfaction with her role and the Foreign Service lifestyle cannot be generalized. Some prefer smaller posts, where the embassy community is close-knit; others prefer large places, where one feels one is less in a fishbowl. Of course, certain European countries are considered very desirable places to live, yet in those countries wives may not have opportunities to become involved in worthwhile volunteer projects such as those described earlier in this chapter. In general, these wives described the vast majority of their posts in glowing terms.

The Lives of Ambassadors' Wives

THE MAJORITY of older generation wives have been "senior wives," meaning that their husbands have held senior positions as ambassador or consul general. While junior wives may see the senior wives as living in the lap of luxury and sometimes as being aloof, wives of principal officers are actually hard workers who are often lonely. All of these women carried out representational responsibilities, and most also volunteered for charitable and women's club activities. A few said such activities were often burdensome; others said they particularly liked to entertain. While it is true that the senior officer at an overseas post (ambassador, consul general, or chargé, who is a temporary principal officer) is usually given a large government-owned residence, a necessity for entertaining, and servants to help run it and care for it, those who have not been in this position may not realize the amount of work such a residence involves. If a wife is fortunate, she has a good housekeeper to run the residence, but at many posts trained and experienced help is not available. The tasks of managing the house and the staff, as well as planning and executing social events, fall to the wives, who are not paid for this work.

Elizabeth Shannon, whose husband served as ambassador to Ireland from 1977 to 1981, wrote in her memoir *Up in the Park*:

> I feel as if I may be in over my head, that I am sinking in a sea of invitations, lists, arrangements, plans, parties, and guests. That I don't know what I am doing from hour to hour. I've got a reception for three hundred members of the Friendship Force from Worcester, Massachusetts, coming up in two weeks, followed by a Fourth of July reception for everyone in Dublin who can walk or talk; I've got eighty women from the Irish Countrywomen's Association coming to tea this afternoon, and a party for the National Press Club, four sets of house guests arriving over the next four weeks, and a black-tie dinner for twenty-four on July 5th.[3]

The following is from Louise, whose husband was ambassador at a particularly important post in the late 1980s:

> Most days I had one, two, or three appointments of some sort at the residence. So I usually had people to tea or coffee most days. I guess it was more unusual than not to have people to breakfast, but if there was no other time to have them we did. We had working lunches several times a week. We tried to keep the weekends as free as we could, and then dinner, I'd say more often than not, we either had very large receptions, or we could seat 120 for dinner, so once a week or so we would do that.

As one can see from these examples, being an ambassador's wife can be, as Greta said, "a full-time job" or, as Jean said, "like running a hotel." Audrey, whose husband reached ambassador level at a relatively young age, said that "you are on a treadmill." And it is not always the glamorous job it seems. Greta arrived at the ambassador's residence, her new home, to find peeling paint and mildewed curtains, so she set about restoring, renovating, and redecorating the house. In addition, they were posted in a developing country where they could not even buy staples such as bread, so she spent hours in the kitchen trying to teach the not-very-well-trained cook to bake. For Greta,

> It was not a glamorous job. It may have looked like that, as once I was ready for the party, of course, I put on a nice dress and I smiled and it looked to my guests like I had just rested (laughs)! They didn't know that I worked all day.

All of these wives said that they were treated differently as ambassador's wife. While an ambassador's wife shares in her husband's status and is accorded deference by the embassy staff and host country nationals, many wives experienced this in a negative way. Jean said,

> They don't basically trust an ambassador's wife because they don't know whether she'll interfere in an ambassador's duties, so the less you can interfere in it the better, I think. I tried to keep my nose out of that. I don't think being an ambassador's wife is as pleasant as the other things that you do in the Service.

The ambassador's wife is treated according to her role, not according to her individual self. Even wives of the deputy chief of mission, the second-highest level, experienced difficulties from their imposed role, as Elaine explains:

> I'm not used to people treating me in a role rather than as myself. It was hard. And I didn't

want to adjust to that, I didn't want to be treated
as a role, instead of as myself.

When one is treated according to one's vicarious status, it
can be difficult to retain a genuine sense of self. Two wives
in particular reflected on the problem of maintaining a
sense of self within the "role":

> There's a real danger, because people bend over
> backward to be nice to you, and want to tell
> you all the good news and keep the bad news
> away, and they want to curry favor with you,
> and it's difficult. We tried very hard not to get
> used to it. But we had four ambassadorial posts
> one right after the other, and it sort of seeps in
> like water. You begin to think you're really quite
> an outstanding person, quite unusual, really, as
> an ambassador's wife, or an ambassador's child;
> "this is the ambassador's son, this is the am-
> bassador's daughter." Yuck! (Alice)

> You get an idea that you are somebody, and of
> course you're not. The house is for the govern-
> ment, the car is for the government. You're an
> instrument of the government. And it's a privi-
> lege. And I think if we don't think of it as a
> privilege, it's not going to work. (Jean)

Therefore, these wives may be treated as local celebrities
because of who their husband is, a situation for which
they may be unprepared.

One serious problem that can result is that of not
knowing whether the people one meets are sincere, which
inhibits possibilities for genuine friendships. Vivian, who
had hardly a negative word about her life in the Foreign
Service, said,

> I think that's probably the hardest thing that
> I've had to deal with in the Foreign Service.
> Because you never know or you're not sure
> whether people like you for your own sake, for

something they see inside you, or whether they are befriending you because your husband is who he is, and you are the wife or the spouse of that individual. Or that you are a part of the American Embassy, or that Americans are wealthy, or that Americans can get you a visa, or that Americans have the inside track to the powerful people in the country. And so for all these reasons, that's always been a concern, and it's been something you have to keep your eyes open about.

Thus Foreign Service wives, and ambassadors' wives in particular, may experience loneliness, as Arlene did:

It's lonely. Because people treat you very differently when you get into that situation. They didn't necessarily know you when you were one of the troops and they assume you've always been some exalted person and they sort of project attitudes onto you. They expect you to be high and mighty or a snob or something. And so you have quite a lot to live down.

One of the roles traditionally associated with the status of ambassador's wife has been leader and caretaker of the American embassy community. These wives talked about feeling responsible for the rest of the American community:

You have a lot more responsibility, especially to the Americans. You feel like you really should have them over for Thanksgiving. You felt more of a responsibility for the community.

[I asked, "And did you feel that people appreciated everything you did?"]

I think that some people expected it. (Lynn)

A majority of the respondents in the 1985 *Report on the Role of the Spouse* felt that the ambassador's wife should provide a leadership role in the American community overseas. Others agree. Betty, who is not an ambassador's wife, said,

> I also think that the ambassador's wife, even though she is never paid for it, has a certain responsibility to the American community, to the embassy community. I really think it's something that has to be done. And we certainly have been in places where the ambassador's wife didn't do anything to promote the welfare of the people who were working at the embassy. And I really think that's terrible, and yes, it made me very cross. I really think that even though it's not a paid position it is a real responsibility as a human being that you take care of the people around you. And it's her responsibility and if she doesn't do it, it won't get done.

Arlene's early experiences with other ambassadors' wives greatly affected how she later comported herself as ambassador's wife:

> I became much more conscientious about those things [representational activities] when I was an ambassador's wife because I had been to places where the ambassador's wife was either nonfunctioning or was dysfunctional, and that was worse. That's quite hard on a community. I don't blame the community for having expectations of the people at the top, and I think the wife can make things quite a lot better, by doing certain community things, and can make things quite a lot worse, by malfunctioning in the job.

This ambassador's wife, then, as did others, saw herself as having a real "job," which she took seriously, no matter how vicarious and imposed it may have been. She had observed how others before her had performed in this role. When her turn came, she saw it as an opportunity to make a contribution, specifically by improving community life at post. Thus ambassadors' wives face enormous demands to step into ready-made positions at overseas posts.

In some posts it has been traditional for the wife of the ambassador to become the honorary president of the women's (or wives') association. Vivian said that it was assumed that as the wife of the American ambassador, she would serve as president of the women's organization at their post:

> It was a charitable organization, and they were waiting for me to arrive, because they knew that the American ambassador was coming with a wife. And I heard this, months before, that they were waiting for me to become president of the organization. So when I got there I had an answer for them. My concern was that I really didn't want to move into a job and/or position when I had just arrived in the country. I really wanted to be able to put down some roots, to travel a bit, to see as much as I could, and to make a decision as to the kinds of projects and programs that I wanted to become involved in. So it made sense to them, but they still lobbied very hard. So I told them that I wouldn't take the presidency, and that was fine, but what I did assume was the chairman of social welfare, which is the charitable arm of the organization. [She later did become president.]

Another serious problem these women encountered was the threat of danger. High-ranking American officials abroad are often targets of terrorism. The heavy security given to ambassadors and their families can feel like a severe invasion of privacy. Audrey remembers a European post in the mid-1980s in positive terms, except that "my only negative then was the security and the terrorist threat which sometimes I would really get into a white panic about." Arlene said that at one post, "my husband was identified [as] target number one."

Of course, there are benefits to being the wife of an ambassador. One does get to travel to interesting places and meet important people. One feels a certain amount of status and prestige. Others may look to one as a role model (which can be both an honor and a burden). Greta, the German-born wife, told me,

One thing is nice, because you get a lot of respect as an ambassador's wife. People listen. I
have a low voice and I can be at a cocktail party
and start a sentence and you know, maybe I
don't even finish it. But when you're an
ambassador's wife, people listen, they let you
finish a sentence, or whatever you want to say.

In the past, when her husband was a lower-level officer,
Greta had received little attention in social settings. She
now appreciates the benefit of the deference that her vicarious role as ambassador's wife brings.

Having servants can, of course, also be an advantage.
Wives of higher-ranking Foreign Service officers are freed
from basic drudgery. However, several of these wives told
me that instead of being helpful, servants actually created
problems. A few had servants who stole from them. Others
weren't comfortable with having non-family members constantly in their homes. As noted earlier, a great deal of time
often had to be spent training household help, so that in
the end the wife would have been better off performing the
tasks herself. Others found themselves having to settle dis-
putes between servants. In addition, wives often felt a personal responsibility for the people who worked for them
overseas. Jean said that while coming back to their average-
sized suburban home in Washington was something of a
comedown, "on the other hand it's nice not to have all
those people's lives in your hands."

I was told of two instances in which ambassadors who
did not have wives present at post were given a special
paid assistant to perform the activities normally carried
out by a wife, which shows that the work the ambassador's
wife does is real and considered important enough that a
person may be hired to fill that place if a wife is absent. (In
one case, the wife was a Foreign Service officer who did
not join her husband at his post; in the other case, the
ambassador was unmarried.)

Disparate Views of the '72 Directive

THE DIRECTIVE of 1972, as explained earlier, proclaimed
that wives were private persons and would no longer be

required to perform any services for the United States government. Some wives of the older generation, who served in the pre-1972 Foreign Service, have not been entirely happy with the change. Maude, an ambassador's wife who is proud of her accomplishments as a Foreign Service wife, told me,

> I think they wanted allowances for the stuff they were doing that was of value. They didn't argue allowances, though, which they probably could have gotten. They argued instead that women should not be under other women. Of course, none of these things were exactly true. So the '72 Directive, which said a woman is a free agent, she is not a chattel of the government, she can't be forced to do anything, was true anyway. That was true. Nobody could *force* wives to do anything.

Maude, who has freely and willingly given her time and energy over the years, believes that the issue of spousal compensation was what really needed to be addressed but was not. Instead, the focus was the wives' hierarchies. Maude says of dragon ladies, "There weren't any." Also, in contrast with other wives, Maude claims that it was never true that wives could be forced to do anything they didn't want to, and thus the '72 Directive was really moot. While it may be that wives could not be *forced* to participate, many clearly felt the pressure to do so.

Sophie, who also paid close attention to the discussions that led to the '72 Directive, told me that the board of the American Association of Foreign Service Women (AAFSW) was actually against the proposal because

> They saw it very much as undermining what they had done. One of the things that it did was say that wives could no longer be part of the efficiency report. And I think most of them had been model wives, and they really felt that they had had a major role to play in their husband's career, and that his success had something to do with what they had done. And they saw being

in his efficiency report as recognition of what
they had done.

Indeed, some wives did like being written about in their
husbands' evaluations, because it was a way of being recognized. Maude said,

> Behind it all, I knew I was an asset. I knew I was
> good (laughs). In fact, the only criticism I had
> is that they didn't say enough! No, I was always
> in there. I was probably in those days much more
> ambitious than my husband.

Thus, many traditional wives believed themselves to
be legitimate and useful members of a team; they fully
embraced their role as part of a two-person career. They
therefore perceived the '72 Directive as taking away that
role. The State Department had told them that their work
on behalf of diplomacy was as important as their husband's;
now, after receiving their full commitment, the Department was telling them they were not, after all, part of the
team. It is not surprising that some women were resent-
ful. Others, like Alice, defensively took the attitude that
the Directive was meaningless:

> That airgram on the status of spouses, I thought
> it was a bunch of nonsense, and the spouses
> didn't even like it! It said that you had no du-
> ties or responsibilities to the U.S. government,
> even though you're a government spouse. Well,
> I think that's rubbish, because if you're living
> in a rent-free housing unit of some kind, that
> automatically gives you an obligation in my
> book. Some people thought you were such a
> plus accompanying your husband, that was part
> of the deal, and that you didn't have to do any-
> thing in return for it. So it was a rather unhealthy
> attitude, that you had no obligations. So I never
> bought it and then I discovered that the wives
> didn't like it because it meant they were out of
> it, they were out of the loop and they didn't
> know what was going on anymore and it wasn't
> any fun. It was to protect them against dragon

lady wives, who bullied them into making five
hundred stuffed eggs for the fourth of July.

Wives like Alice took their obligations as part of a two-
person Foreign Service career seriously. Most of the older
wives don't believe for a minute that they are really "private persons" with no responsibilities toward the American government. Emma, whose husband became an
ambassador, perfectly illustrates the feelings of the older
generation:

> I knew that what I did was important, and that
> the effort had to be shared to a large degree,
> and that he needed my support, and I wanted
> to be supportive. I liked feeling a part of what
> he was doing. And it was very much a joint ef-
> fort. And he has said that you can't really be
> representative without having the combined ef-
> fort. And of course there are fine Foreign Ser-
> vice officers who are single people and don't
> have a family around to support them and por-
> tray the typical American family. But if you are a
> family, it would be a disaster if you didn't, I
> think. And I think it works better if there are
> two of you involved. And then the people that
> he worked with, it was always helpful for me to
> know their wives and to let them know that I
> enjoyed being in their country. It was something
> that I wanted to do, and I felt a part of it, repre-
> senting America. It sounds too noble, doesn't it?

According to Sophie, it was a group of younger wives
(some of whom are now the "older" women of this chapter) who demanded the changes, for the following reason:

> When you went overseas, and you had ambassa-
> dors' wives telling you to show up and set the
> table, or to leave your kids at home with some
> babysitter that you didn't know, so that you
> could make three hundred tea sandwiches for
> their reception and then you didn't get in-
> vited.... They simply said, you know, no thanks,
> I don't want any part of this. And there was just

enough of that, that those people who felt they'd really been abused all came together and said, no more, we're tired of this two-for-the-price-of-one. We're independent, we don't work for the State Department, the State Department doesn't pay us, and we're not going to do it anymore.

Sophie was involved with the AAFSW at the time of these discussions, and describes definite (and antagonistic) generational divisions among the women. Most older women felt that the '72 Directive was enacted to free younger wives from the tyranny of older ones. By refusing to perform such tasks anymore, younger women were signaling to older women that this work was neither important nor fulfilling. The older wives saw value in the work they had been doing, while the younger spouses either saw none or at least wanted a choice in the matter.

This issue of division between generations is raised repeatedly. Renate, who has been involved with Foreign Service activities throughout the course of these changes, sees the younger women as part of the "me generation." She believes there is a real problem with the younger women; in her eyes all they do is complain about Foreign Service life. They do not appreciate the positive changes that her generation helped to bring about. They just "want it all," she says; what they have, "It's not enough, but it's not so bad!"

Marital Problems and Midlife Crises

ALL THE women, when asked if they had had marital problems that were directly due to the Foreign Service, said, for the most part, no. Some mentioned the stress and strain that moving can place on relationships. A few cited arguments over entertaining, with the wife wishing to entertain less frequently than her husband wanted her to. For example, Greta had returned to school and was busy with her studies, yet at the same time her husband insisted that she give frequent parties for his colleagues.

The ambassadors' wives in particular tended to have experienced periods of crisis when they were severely dissatisfied with their lives. Sometimes the crisis was set off by conditions overseas, while in other cases the catalyst was returning to the United States. One observer has noted that many diplomatic wives feel the marriage they have overseas is different from the one they have at home.[4] For example, one wife felt useless and ignored by her husband when they returned to the United States after she had played her role beautifully abroad. For the women who felt periods of crisis, it appears that their husbands were more career-oriented than some of the other husbands. The word "workaholic" was used more than once. I also heard complaints that the women felt that they had raised their children all by themselves. In each case, the crisis ended when the wife found something fulfilling of her own to do, such as returning to an earlier goal and trying to fulfill it, finding a job, or returning to school.

The most consistently happy marriages were those in which the husbands were more family- than career-oriented. Several of the husbands had made sacrifices for their families, such as putting off overseas postings so their children could complete high school in the United States or retiring early to spend more time with their families. On the other hand, some couples had lived through separations; while the officer went off to his overseas assignment, the wife remained in the United States in order for their child(ren) to finish school or so that she could pursue a job. In some other cases wives were not allowed to join their husbands at, or were evacuated from, dangerous overseas posts. These separations were in all cases difficult for families, and the wives who had endured such situations said they never wished to again.

Questions of Identity

MANY OF the points discussed in this book, such as being part of a "two-person career," having a "derived role," and "achieving vicariously," are identity-related. But many of the older generation of Foreign Service wives had difficulty answering questions about their identity. Some said they were unsure; others said they had no identity or that it was changing or situational, or that they were "looking for a new one." Of the rest, several mentioned their current job, though not as determining their whole identity.

Some of the ambiguity about identity was because of
the lack of continuity in Foreign Service life. Some have
felt a positive identity as a Foreign Service wife, but with
their husbands now retired they feel the loss of that identity. Most have a paying job, but haven't held it long
enough to identify themselves with it. Still others have
filled their lives with a multitude of different activities,
whether volunteer or paid, leaving them with no central
way of defining themselves.

This was not a problem for some, who happily told
me they were "many things." For others, however, not
having a central, accepted way of defining themselves was
problematic because of feeling judged by others. For example, the youngest of these women, Elaine, whose husband is still an active officer, said,

> I'm really a strange bird, in Foreign Service
> circles or in almost any circle at this point, be-
> cause almost all of the wives of the people with
> whom we associate have a profession. And they
> ask me what I do, and I say, "Well, I do volun-
> teer work, right now I've been working on our
> house...." And they sort of look at me like, oh,
> that's nice.

While the Foreign Service experience has been a pleasant
one for Elaine, she is uncomfortable with being such a
"strange bird" and is currently looking for a new activity
to give meaning to her life.

Arlene began her life focused on her husband and
family but later on was able to begin a successful career
connected to her Foreign Service experiences. Concerning her early family-oriented years, she told me,

> I feel very lucky in a way because I never had
> the feeling that I should be doing something
> else. In my day it was perfectly all right to have
> children and look after your children. It was as-
> sumed that you were the best person to look af-
> ter your children. I happen to think that often
> that's true. I don't think people have a real choice

nowadays. I think people are in a big bind about, you know, work and family obligations.

Arlene knows that an educated women who describes herself as "wife and mother" may suffer some stigma today. Elaine blames this situation on the feminist movement, which she feels belittles the choices of traditional women like her:

> I'm not particularly happy with where the feminist movement has left people like me. I feel like women should do what they feel is right for them and they should have absolutely equal opportunity with everybody else, to do what they're suited to do, whatever that may be. But I feel like the woman who dedicates herself to raising children who feel loved and cared for deserves an equal amount of respect with the woman who decides that what she best does is something else.

"An Odd Résumé"

THE MAJORITY of the traditional women I interviewed have held paying jobs overseas. Many worked as teachers, while others found employment within embassies. When the Department of State created the Family Liaison Office in 1978, family liaison officers (now called community liaison officers, or CLOs) were appointed at posts overseas. While the special needs of any given post determine the CLO's duties, in general she or he is concerned with the well-being of employees and their families overseas. From the beginning these positions were made available to spouses, and four wives in this group have served as CLOs overseas.

All of the women interviewed for this chapter have worked in paying jobs in the United States. Currently the majority have professions: some are in elementary or university teaching, a few are writers, and others are engaged in international work at the State Department or elsewhere. Of the rest, two are very involved with volunteer activities,

one is looking for full-time work, and one just began a
new job at the Department of State. Elaine, who described
herself as a "strange bird," is looking for something new
to do, whether paid or volunteer work. She told me,

> You know, when you've spent so many years of
> your life doing volunteer work and doing vari-
> ous unpaid things, which are important and tax-
> ing but for which you haven't been compensated
> at all monetarily, it makes sort of an odd résumé.
> And I haven't really sat down and put it all to-
> gether in résumé form, which I should do. I've
> done some fairly tough things over the years.
> But putting them into a form which will be im-
> pressive to a prospective employer—And I'm
> completely computer nonliterate. So I'm an
> anachronism in the job market. I don't really fit
> into what's going on in the economic world.

This illustrates one major disadvantage that comes from
being geographically mobile: lack of continuity in one's
work life, paid professional or volunteer.

All of the women in this chapter can be characterized
as generally happy and satisfied with their lives. Those who
enjoyed Foreign Service life the most are those who felt
(and still feel) a strong identification with the Service: they
made a "profession" out of being a Foreign Service wife
and were able to translate their overseas experience and/or
connection with the U.S. government into fascinating careers. Some have held jobs at the Foreign Service Institute's
Overseas Briefing Center, in training programs for spouses
and families. Others have worked at the Family Liaison Office
(one was director there) or the Foreign Service Lounge,
which also deals with family issues. Others educate or con-
sult on issues of overseas living; for example, one does speak-
ing engagements about her experiences as wife of an
ambassador to an important country.

Other wives had professions that could easily be ac-
commodated within the Foreign Service lifestyle: academic,
teacher, writer. These women are also happy; they have
loved the travel aspect of their husbands' jobs and have
been able to carve out a career for themselves off and on

over the years. Only one wife, Catherine, really regrets being unable to pursue her dream of a career in the fine arts. Yet she admitted that her parents' discouraging her was as important a factor as her husband's career in not achieving her goal. Still, she has been able to be involved in this field as an amateur, which she finds at least partially fulfilling.

A few of these wives positively bubbled over with stories of happy and exciting experiences overseas. For those who never pursued a career of their own, being a part of the Foreign Service was very fulfilling. Margaret, who recently began a job with the Department of State, told me,

> I just want to feel that wherever I go, whatever I do, that I add to wherever I am, I help out, whether it's the church, the school, the embassy, or a little of each. And that's always been what's made me really happy. Because at the end of the road, it's not how much money you've made. To me it's the friendships, the moments, the associations. At the end of the road you can be very happy about a profession, but I've just seen too many people retire and get a fifty-year pin and walk out the door to nothing. Because they've worked their whole life and they've never explored another side.... So for me it was never important to have my career. For me the Foreign Service is ideal, it's just given me a wonderfully rich opportunity to meet a whole bunch of different people.... I would wish anyone to have as wonderful a life.

"Alice"

THE BEST example of a wife in the older generation is Alice. We met in her home, which was beautifully decorated with art objects from all over the world. She was obviously preparing for a dinner party that evening. Alice grew up in a middle-class family in the Midwest; her mother worked only during the Depression. Alice graduated from college with a degree in history but said the extent of her ambition was to work for a year or two before marriage. While she was dating her husband-to-be in the late 1950s, he took the Foreign Service examinations and passed them, and she was pleased because she wanted to travel.

Overseas she helped wherever she could, became involved in volunteer activities, enjoyed the traveling and moving, and was always curious to see what was around the next corner. She told me she loved entertaining: "I love giving parties and if someone's prepared to reimburse me, I think that's terrific." She liked being written up on her husband's efficiency report because she saw it as positive recognition of her work. While she doesn't feel that she should have been paid for her years of work as a Foreign Service wife, she does wish that she could collect her own pension because she emphasizes that everyone should have some means of financial security and independence.

One thing that Alice minded was that her husband was (and still is, she says) a workaholic. He was mostly absent when it came to raising the children, which she said was a problem. The biggest difficulty in her life came when they were posted in Washington, D.C., after service overseas. The reverse culture shock is the worst, she told me, because suddenly she did not have a role to play. During one period in Washington her husband had to travel two-thirds of the time, leaving her at home with nothing to do. She had returned to Washington to find unhappily that "I had skills that were not in demand. Nobody needed dinner parties given, people called on." Her husband was working or traveling all the time "and just seemed to forget about me, and all the help I had been to him overseas." She discovered, with some surprise, that all her friends had paying jobs.

After floundering around most unhappily for a couple of years, she used her international experience and connections to find a job at an international foundation. Her job brought her the self-respect she needed. Yet when her husband retired from the Foreign Service and moved to another state to take a new job, she left her position to follow him again. She now says that she is looking for a new identity, because she doesn't have one as a Foreign Service wife anymore. Overall, though, she was very happy when they were posted overseas and her husband's work was hers, also.

Conclusion: Committed Wives

COMMITMENT IS a term that summarizes the attitude of the older women to their husbands and to their husbands' profession. They were generally happy to commit themselves to their husbands' career and took satisfaction in the contributions they made as unpaid partners. In accordance with what one wife has written, they feel they have "led useful lives."[5] Many are very proud of the difficulties they have lived through and look upon themselves as being unique because they have lived special, different lives. Commitment is what these wives see lacking in the newer generations of Foreign Service officers and spouses, and they are disdainful of them:

> I just grimace when I hear these young women that are coming in. I haven't heard it so much from men, and I've been around a lot of male spouses, but you know, "Well, I never expected this, I'm only doing this for the ride, I'm only going to do this for a short period of time." And I guess commitment is what's lacking. (Margaret)

Those of the older generation observe that the newer one is different:

> What one notices that's different, we signed on as a lifelong profession, and nowadays, many more people are in-and-outers, or they say they're going to be outers—I'm not sure if the economy allows them to be. (Arlene)

The 1985 survey of spouses reported that 96 percent of spouses of senior Foreign Service officers said they believe that fewer spouses are now willing to participate in unpaid representational work. In the next chapter I discuss my findings from a group of younger wives to gauge if the older wives' view of them as "uncommitted" is an apt one.

NOTES

1. Betty Sowers Alt and Bonnie Domrose Stone, *Campfollowing: A History of the Military Wife* (New York: Praeger, 1991); Bonnie Domrose Stone and Betty Sowers Alt, *Uncle Sam's Brides: The World of Military Wives* (New York: Walker, 1990).

2. This quotation is from a wife who is not included in this chapter's core sample of twenty-one wives. She is no longer a Foreign Service wife (having been widowed), but is now a Foreign Service officer herself. I include her words here because they are relevant to understanding the expectations placed on wives in the old days.

3. Elizabeth Shannon, *Up in the Park: The Diary of the Wife of the American Ambassador to Ireland, 1977-1981* (New York: Atheneum, 1983), p. 273.

4. Cynthia Enloe, *Bananas, Beaches, and Bases: Making Feminist Sense of International Politics* (Berkeley: University of California Press, 1990), p. 102.

5. Jane S. Hart, untitled essay in *Diplomacy: The Role of the Wife,* ed. Martin F. Herz (Washington, D.C.: Georgetown University Institute for the Study of Diplomacy, 1981).

5

The New, Uncommitted Wives

This CHAPTER RELATES THE experiences of twenty-one women newer to the Foreign Service than those described in the previous chapter. At the time of our meetings, these women ranged in age from 27 to 44; their average age was 34. Their husbands had entered the Foreign Service between 1976 and 1990, with two-thirds having entered in the 1980s. Thus, these wives began their Foreign Service experience after the '72 Directive was issued. They had an average of 1.5 children, with the number of children ranging from zero to three. Some of them were still planning to have children, or additional children. Two-thirds described their backgrounds as middle-class, while five were upper-middle-class or from wealthy backgrounds and two come from working-class families. None were poor as children. As with the older group of wives interviewed, two of this younger group were foreign-born.[1]

"You Had a Career, There Was No Question About It"

BECAUSE THE women in this group grew up either during or after the women's movement, one would expect them to have career ambitions, and they did. Two-thirds told me that their initial orientation was toward a career, while only one said she was more family-oriented; the rest told me they never really knew what they wanted to do. Of the total, half of their mothers worked for pay while they were growing up. Sandra, a 38-year-old attorney, told me that because her mother had been a frustrated housewife, she grew up vowing not to stay at home. However, due to her husband's job with the Foreign Service, that was what she was doing:

> And one of the things I grew up with was that I wasn't going to stay home.... Now it's happening to me because of the Foreign Service, and that's kind of weird.... Everyone in college, all my friends, we weren't going to have kids, and we were always going to get jobs. My life is so disconnected now. I have people from [college] that I don't even hear from anymore, and I don't know if it's because I've gone on this other path. A lot of my friends from high school and college never got married or never had kids. There's a lot more career dedication among them. And I was like that but the Foreign Service, partly, pushed me into a different realm, I guess.

Kim, a bright and energetic 29-year-old, described a similar environment at her university:

> I feel like when I went to college, that's just what you did, you had a career, there was no question about it. It doesn't matter if you're a man or a woman, if you're going to college you're going to get out, you're going to have a career, that's what you do.

These statements are quite a contrast to those of the older Foreign Service wives, who were more apt to describe college as a place to meet a husband.

Some who weren't strongly career-oriented at first, including a woman who later became a nurse, said that although they weren't necessarily driven to pursue any particular career, they did feel an urge to leave their hometowns. So this group shared with the older group a desire for adventure and travel.

"Traipsing Around" After Their Husbands

THESE TWENTY-ONE women became Foreign Service wives in any of three ways. Six women married men who were already Foreign Service officers. For them, their love for the men prevailed over their doubts about the lifestyle. Some couples decided together to try the Foreign Service after having had other careers. These wives wanted to take a break from working and have children, or wanted to travel. In the remaining cases, the husbands made a unilateral decision to enter the Foreign Service, and the wives unhappily went along.

Of the six who married Foreign Service officers, four agonized about the two-person career that they knew would come with the marriage. This is very unlike the older wives. For example, Ann, a professional artist, told me, "From what I witnessed in the Foreign Service I didn't want to be a Foreign Service wife. I felt that there were tremendous demands...." Another wife, Beth, is the daughter of a Foreign Service officer, so she was well aware of what being a Foreign Service wife would entail. Also a professional, she never expected to fall in love with a Foreign Service officer:

> We'd known each other for about three years and he had to go overseas. And he went and I didn't go with him the first year. I couldn't make a decision, is probably the better way to put it. I was just really torn. But then I just said, well, what are you going to do? I really cared, loved him, still do very much, and felt this was a really good relationship with the right person, and at the end of my life I didn't want to sit back and say...well, I think I would have felt I'd made the wrong decision.

She viewed his career as a drawback rather than an attraction, but she loved him enough to marry him in spite of it.

Jacqueline spoke about her situation in very matter-of-fact tones; she said her future husband attempted to put a positive "spin" on his career when it was clear that she found it unappealing:

> Well, I've always warned him that I adore to travel more than anything, but I love to do just that, travel, and then come back home. I knew I wouldn't want to live abroad. So he said, "Well, I have a law degree, and at age 50 I can retire and go on to something else. Plus most posts are only two years long...." He knew that I wasn't [interested in living abroad]. But I think he thought he could convince me.

After accompanying her husband to one overseas post, Jacqueline has informed him that the next time he is assigned overseas she will not go with him; she will stay at home with the children and visit him abroad.

Rachel also took an instant dislike to the thought of being married to a diplomat:

> My first thought when I met him and he told me what he did—I liked him—but then when he told me about his job I thought, there's no way I'm going to traipse around after someone my whole life, just following him and his job around. I just thought that was the most repulsive thing in the world. But here I am, doing it.

For these wives, unlike those of the older generation, the decision to marry a Foreign Service officer took a great deal of serious consideration; they saw the man's career as a liability.

For those couples who decided together that the husband should join the Foreign Service, a life of foreign travel was an important incentive, as it was for the older generation. For example, I was told,

> There was that aspect of wanting to branch out and see the world from a bigger picture, and there was also the fact that we like to travel, we like to experience other cultures, and wanted to

have somebody else finance it for a change....
So it was a big adventure. (Amanda)

I thought that this was just an adventure for us.
(Kate)

And it was an adventure, which was what we
wanted. (Cecile)

Another motivating factor for joining the Foreign Service was the opportunity for the wife to take a break from
work. After several years of putting in long hours at their
jobs, some women who had been career-oriented realized
that professional life is not always ideal. They were delighted
that their husbands wanted to join the Foreign Service; this
would give them a break from the breadwinner role. For
example:

I was the one who was actually more eager to
go in. Even though it meant giving up an absolutely wonderful job that I loved. But I'd been
working for eight years, I'd even had the start
of an ulcer years back, I had a baby that I wasn't
home with, although not that I want to be home
or wanted to be home all the time with babies,
but I just thought it was a great adventure and
I was ready. (Christine)

Kim, who did not have children yet, was already discontented with the working world:

It's like we all planned on having this career, but
then we got out of college and we got in the
working world and first of all it was the first time
I ever experienced sexual discrimination.... I got
really disillusioned because it was always the political thing at the office.... And I don't live to
work. I want to work and keep busy, but my job
is not my life.... I like to travel, I like to do other
things too much.... So I just felt really fed up,
you know. And so my husband said, you know,

"If I get into the Foreign Service, you can take a break, you can think about what you want to do."

For some, taking a break from the working world also meant the opportunity to have children:

> And so I gave up my career, a very lucrative pay-ing job. And the other thing was that I wanted to have a baby and I didn't see how I could stay in my previous job because I worked long hours and I traveled a lot and I didn't see how I could raise a child the way I wanted to and stay in that job. So it just sort of happened that the Foreign Service called...at the right time, and we decided to make this big change. (Amanda)

For women who wish to have children, Foreign Service life can make a great deal of sense; because job opportuni-ties overseas are usually lacking, wives are in effect forced to stay home and raise their children. Also, in many parts of the world household help and child care are available for little money. In contrast, being part of a dual-career couple in the United States often means little time for one's children and expensive day care bills. Therefore, many in this younger group of wives use their time in the For-eign Service as an opportunity to have and raise children.

In contrast to the wives who chose the Foreign Service, other wives were surprised by their husband's decision to join. Elizabeth, a 44-year-old with three chil-dren, said,

> In fact, one of the things that attracted me to him so strongly was that he seemed so sturdy and stable.... And then two years after we were married...he came to me and he said, "I finally know what I want to do with my life.... I want to be in the Foreign Service." What's that? "Oh, you're a diplomat, and you go to world capitals and you're a VIP and you travel all over the place and associate with the crème de la crème." It sounded great...I said, "Okay."

Elizabeth was initially agreeable but became more miserable with the lifestyle as the years progressed. She discovered that she could not continue to pursue her career in the performing arts as she thought she would be able to. She considered ending the marriage but eventually decided to remain with her husband.

Similarly, Jan's husband proceeded with his career choice without really discussing it with her. A teacher, Jan unhappily acquiesced, and years later she still feels a sense of unreality about it all:

> So truly, I knew nothing about the Foreign Service. I knew nothing about this test he was taking. And I really didn't question that. Because in my mind, it was something that he felt the need to do, to feel a sense of achievement.... Then he passed.... He talked to them, they called him.... So by the time he came home from work and I came home from work he had already said yes, yes, that he wanted to do this. And I thought, what is he talking about?

Marjorie, a graduate student, was also surprised when her husband informed her that he had taken and passed the examination:

> We talked about it, we argued about it.... And I think probably if I had known, although hindsight's always twenty–twenty, isn't it? If I had known really what it was going to be like, I would have put up a lot more resistance than I did at the outset. Also he said to me things like, it was something he wanted to at least try for awhile, and if it looked like it wasn't going to work out, then he would think about doing something else. He talks a good game, but he basically likes what he does and he's very successful at it.

Elizabeth, Jan, and Marjorie all expressed deep unhappiness over their husband's choice, and they laughed at

themselves in disbelief at the unwanted situation in which
they still found themselves.

Image was part of the problem for some wives. Those
who had any impression at all of the Foreign Service prior
to their joining it, thought of it as upper-crust:

> I had this image that…all diplomats were stuffy.
> And he was more, closer to hippie, the way he
> dressed. (Yasmin)

> I had an image that all the other wives would be
> very proper and very…I don't know, come from
> upper-class backgrounds and stuff and I was kind
> of curious what they would be like. And the first
> spouse I met had been the only female world
> class Formula One motorcycle racer in the world.
> (Randi)

> I guess I grew up with this view of the Foreign
> Service as a glamorous kind of life, and I think
> possibly that's a good word for it, because it's a
> lot of illusion. There's this *appearance* of ex-
> citement…. (Teresa)

As I describe in the next section, these women learned
quickly that the image was not the reality.

"We Call It Being 'Spoused'"

LIKE THE older wives, these wives learned early on how
they would be treated and about their role as Foreign Service wives. Just over half of the wives of this group attended classes at the Foreign Service Institute upon their
husbands' entry into the Foreign Service. In an FSI language class, Amanda, whose husband entered the Foreign
Service in 1990, soon discovered what her status as a spouse
was to be:

> I found that in my language training they treated
> the spouses differently. At first I tried to deny
> that that was going on. But it was real obvious

> to me and since then I've heard other women
> talk about it.... So they have a tendency to treat
> us a little bit like second-class citizens.... And
> they don't have to do anything for the wives, so
> they sort of see it as, well, we'll do you a favor
> and let you come to these classes but we don't
> have to if we don't want to.... We call it being
> "spoused" (laughs), being treated a little bit like
> second-class citizens.

Sandra, who had taken and passed the Foreign Service
examination herself but had decided to forgo professional
life while she had a baby, told a story about registering for
a language course, along with other spouses. Some had
resigned their jobs to take this course. The Foreign Service Institute suddenly announced that the classes were
overbooked and that no spouses could be enrolled. Furi-
ous, Sandra wrote a letter to the director of the Institute
to complain, and eventually all the spouses were accom-
modated. As she pointed out,

> The idea that spouses' language training isn't
> that important, that's another thing that makes
> me so angry because you're the one that has to
> go shopping, you're the one that has to do all
> this stuff, you're the one who has to go to cock-
> tail parties where you don't know anybody at
> all and have to talk to these people from all these
> other countries. And speak to the neighbors.

Linda, who has a master's degree in library science,
was really startled by what she learned at the Overseas
Briefing Center, the part of the Foreign Service Institute
that develops and conducts programs for families going
overseas:

> I hadn't really thought about the wife's role as
> an entertainer. I had not thought of myself as a
> partner. I thought, this was his job.... I certainly
> hadn't thought of myself as an unpaid append-
> age. But I went to the Overseas Briefing Center

and there were some quite nice women, but
there was a woman who gave a lecture on how
badly we could scotch our husband's career by
insisting on our independence.

This occurred more than a decade after the '72 Directive,
which declared that spouses were private people with no
obligations towards the U.S. government. Official policy
contradicts the reality—wives are still expected to serve as
unpaid Foreign Service employees.

Wives also feel that the work involved in moving is
assumed to be part of their role as "wife of." A Foreign
Service career can mean that every few years there is packing and unpacking, and I found that these chores most
often fall to the wife. Sandra told me,

And there's really an assumption on the part of
the bureaucracy that I am here to just move. That
he gets two days off on either end.... So he's had
two days off to move into the house. And there I
am with millions of boxes and these two kids have
got to live there, and somebody's got to unpack
them. You can't live there. And if I had a job I
suppose we'd do it on the weekends, but there I
am, thanks to the Foreign Service I have no job,
thanks to the Foreign Service I'm just sitting
around unpacking boxes. It seems to me that if
more people weren't married they would have
more days off or something.

In Sandra's estimation, the government does not allow
her husband sufficient time off to take care of the packing
and unpacking chores that come with his job; rather, it is
assumed that she is at home to attend to these matters.

Other respondents told tales about their first experiences at posts abroad, which taught them that wives are
still expected to perform certain duties. Ann, the artist
whose husband was already a Foreign Service officer when
she married him, described how she felt upon arrival, in
the late 1980s, at a post where her husband was to serve
in a high position:

Initially I was floored and overwhelmed. Just stunned by what was expected of me, in that it's a very tiny fishbowl society. I stepped off the plane [and] you're just surrounded by people and everybody wants to be your friend, and everybody wants to know you, and everybody wants you to come to dinner and lunch, and everybody feels a sense of added value in their life for having spent lunch with you. It was just bizarre to me.... And to me it was ridiculous because it really was not substantive. It did not assist my husband in his work and it did not help me.... The second day I was there I was upstairs and all of the sudden I heard somebody playing the piano downstairs. And here was the president of the American Women's Club who just walked in and sat down, unannounced! And I sat down and she sat there and read me twenty-five things that would be required of me. I must do this, I must do that, that we expect this, you do this....

I asked Ann if she had carried out the things demanded of her and she said that she felt that she had no choice—she could not say no.

As it was for the older generation of wives, then, demands to participate in community activities are placed upon the new, younger wives. Linda told me,

There the ambassador had a party and we wives were told what jobs we were going to do. [By whom?] Well in this case...it was the cultural affairs officer, my husband's boss at the time.... They all got together and assigned us little duties. Who were we to say, no thanks!

I asked Linda if she knew that officially she wasn't required to do anything, and she said,

I knew that but at the time it just wasn't important. You're unsure of yourself, you're in a new

profession and a new country, and your tendency
is to go along.... In fact in this case the consul
general's wife was just a lunatic.... Because she
would yell at the FSNs (Foreign Service Nationals, host country citizens employed by the embassy) in front of their subordinates, she would
yell at the officers in front of the FSNs, she yelled
at me in front of the international community!

An older wife would say that Linda had met up with a
"dragon lady." The experiences of these younger women
indicate that not much has really changed since the "old
days" of the Foreign Service.

It is also apparent that in the "new" Foreign Service
what a wife does (or does not do) is still talked about by
others and thus still matters to others. When Ann chose
to spend the bulk of her time on her own work, the result
was surprising to her:

In the end there was this feeling that I was just
rejecting, somehow, the community. I could not
understand why I mattered so much. Why what
I did to fulfill my personal life and needs mattered so much in this community, when to them
it was chit-chatting and breaking bread with a
bunch of women who were always the same....
I remember there was this real frustration on
many people's part with me.

Ann did not let other people's feelings and opinions inter-
fere with how she spent her time. Some wives were able to
adopt this attitude, yet others were not as strong in the face
of gossip and the continuing perception that what the wife
does has an effect on her husband's career. Kate, whose
husband had had two overseas assignments, said,

Even though they no longer do the evaluations
of spouses, I don't think there's any question that
what a spouse does, and more importantly how
she does it...has an effect on her husband's work
within the embassy. They all communicate.

People think of it as this glamorous life. It's not all glamour…it's hard…sometimes you feel like you're back in high school with the…"she did this, she did that."

Ann has the final word on the role of the Foreign Service wife as perceived by the new wives themselves. She summarized her observations of how Foreign Service life affected employees and spouses differently:

I also felt that it was unfair, in that here are these men who are very stimulated by their profession…it was…always something interesting coming along, picking up every three or four years, and retraining and new people, and it was as if they were constantly educating and improving themselves. Where the women seemed to be picking up the tail end of it somehow.

Isolation and Misery

IN CONTRAST to spouses who felt that they were expected to participate immediately, several felt isolated upon arrival in their new country of residence. A study of thirty couples who moved for the sake of the husband's career showed that the wife faced three significant problems following the move: the loss of her usual and accustomed roles; feelings of invisibility and insignificance in the new location; and her husband's lack of attention to her because of his preoccupation with his new workplace.[2] Several of the wives I studied said that their husbands disappeared into the embassy almost immediately after arriving. These wives complained that they were left pretty much alone to fend for themselves in their new surroundings; for example:-

The day we landed he went to the embassy and I didn't see him until seven o'clock. That was that. He was happy as a clam…. The men were so happy, got to their post and off they went.

And we were sort of left. There I am, what do I
do? And when you get to a place and you can't
speak the language and you don't know where
you are, and you don't have a car, what do you
do? And the husband thinks, well, here, this is a
cultural experience for her, she should be so
happy that I've brought her to ——, now it's
up to her to go and have a great time.... I did, I
had a wonderful four years, but I'm not willing
to do that again. (Jacqueline)

This experience was echoed by Jan:

As soon as you get there, you are dropped into
a situation and they go off to the embassy. I
mean the first Monday that you are at a post,
they're gone. They almost can't wait to get into
the embassy to see what their job is, to see what's
going on. They enter a world of people speak-
ing English, and for all intents and purposes
they're in Washington, D.C., in a building in a
foreign country. You are sitting at home in a
foreign situation. You don't know anyone, you
don't speak the language. You have children that
have to have something to do, so you have to
get out right away to figure out who they can
play with, or where they go to school, or all
those kinds of things.... You still have to deal
with all the things in the house that need to be
fixed, with packing and unpacking the boxes.
And it's really frightening. Because you're kind
of lost. You can call the embassy but he's busy.
So you're kind of like, God, I'm alone!

My research supports the above study's finding that after
a move, when the wives needed their husbands most, the
husbands were least available.

Other women felt invisible and ignored after their
overseas move, not only by their husbands but by their
new community. Marjorie, who did not support her
husband's decision to join the Foreign Service, felt stranded

in the small European city where her husband was posted to a tiny consulate. There was no community liaison officer to gather people together for friendship and support. She said she received attention from no one:

> Generally I'm happy not to have those obligations, but...I wouldn't be there if they hadn't sent my husband there. And they seem to think that because you're not required to push cookies anymore, because your husband's not going to be evaluated on the quality of your dinner parties any longer, therefore they seem to think they have no responsibilities toward you or your welfare. Which I disagree with. I mean, I think they've got to have some kind of community and family support.

In contrast to some of the women who felt that demands were made upon them as wives in a two-person career, this wife had little contact with other Americans. She wished for some means of meeting other people, such as community activities, a wives' group, or a support network. Those social structures were lacking for her. The availability of such social structures varies from post to post.

Several wives said that they had endured periods of being wholly miserable at posts abroad. For example:

> There were periods I was miserable. Because it's such a change, to go from where every day you're working and you have too much to do, to nothing. It's just so weird. I left one week and I stopped working and I packed up and I got there and all of the sudden I had nothing to do. It was like, what happened? (Beth)

> I was miserable. I was really miserable. I was like, this is a big mistake. I quit a job I really like, I have a small child...we were living in a house they were giving up the lease on because ours wasn't ready, so it was just a dump, just roach city. I was so miserable, the telephone

> didn't work.... I would just cry, cry, cry, I want
> to go home, I want to go home. (Lisa)

Thus, an overseas move can evoke loneliness, a sense of
loss, boredom, or homesickness.

Does the Representational Role of the Wife Continue?

IN CONTRAST to the wives of the previous generation,
some wives in this group did not participate in representational activities at post. Sixteen women said they
had, and of those, a minority said they did not particularly like entertaining, they tried to limit it, or they felt
pressured into doing it. The rest said they had participated in very few or no social functions. However, this
might be explained by the fact that some of their husbands are still very junior and they are not yet expected
to entertain.

Only Sarah, who had grown up overseas, mentioned
patriotism, which was so important to the older generation, as a reason to entertain:

> I'm more than happy to entertain. A lot of this
> is, you know, your duty, your patriotic duty, how
> you feel about your country and how you want
> it to be represented.... I feel very strongly about
> that.

Almost none of these younger women, then, viewed entertaining and other representational activities as serving
their country. Overall, participating in representational,
volunteer, and other activities at posts abroad has become
more of a personal choice for wives who want to support
their husbands—patriotism is not a factor. This is illus-
trated by the following quotation from Kim:

> Sometimes I think it's not a matter of what you
> want to do for the government but what you
> want to do to support your spouse, and if your
> spouse asks you to, it's one thing. But if some-
> body *expects* you to.... There was stuff that the

ambassador's wife had that I didn't go to. Huh uh. If I don't want to go, I'm not going. As long as it does not hurt his career to a great extent, I'm going to make my own choice.

According to Jan, who has always taught school full-time, the role of the wife has not changed. She said,

There are women Foreign Service officers, but there aren't a whole lot of women in the Foreign Service and I think it still is almost that sexist sort of thing that it's the wife's job to organize the household and give the little dinner parties and to do this, just because you're supposed to do it. You could sit down and converse with everyone at the dinner table but ultimately your job is to make sure everything in the household's running smoothly. And I don't see that that's going to change.

However, two of the wives in this group reported that their husbands shared the responsibility for entertaining equally and performed fully half of the work involved, which was something that I had not heard from any of the older generation of wives.

Still, as stated earlier, it appears that wives continue to be expected to entertain and find themselves the subject of gossip if they do not. For example:

I know the DCM's wife in —— while I was there didn't entertain very much. And people didn't like her and resented her for not opening her house more. But she worked full-time. And I kept thinking, the rules are she's not supposed to have to do this, so why is everybody so mad at her? (Sandra)

From Amanda I heard this:

We were in a post that was really overworked and understaffed and we had, while we were there in two years, eight Secretary of State visits. And it just really saps all the resources of the embassy, everybody has to work. And the wives that would not, it was kind of held against them a little bit. We were disappointed in them, I think, because we needed their help so desperately and they just wouldn't do it.... Everybody was expected to volunteer, and when you didn't it was sort of like, jeez, shock, we could really use your help. So yeah, they got talked about a little bit, not really, I can't say in a vindictive way, but more out of disappointment.

A few of those who met the expectations resented working hard with no compensation for their labor:

I got really angry, I had hired a cook.... I borrowed a cook and he didn't show up. And so I had a small baby, a fifteen-month-old, and I had to put on a dinner party for twenty-five people. And I could have paid an African guy fifty dollars to come in and cook for me, and the embassy would have paid it. But for me doing it, free. There's no money. And that's when it started to bother me. (Randi)

Because you're going to do it anyway. Somehow you're going to get forced into it. The people who don't usually end up leaving post. Everyone talks about them. You're going to end up doing it, is the way I look at it. So sure, why not get reimbursed for it? (Lisa)

For official functions, officers or their wives may hire help, provided that sufficient money is budgeted to do so. However, wives cannot pay themselves when they do the work themselves.

As with the older wives, I asked these women if they had hired servants while they lived overseas, and if so, whether the experience had been positive or negative. Of the twenty-one, sixteen had engaged servants, and of these, seven, or almost half, reported problems. Cecile, a

French-born wife, and Teresa, a dedicated mother of two, said that the servants stole from them. One wife, Lisa, reported that the employees were often a cause of arguments between herself and her husband, while another, Barbara, felt that having servants is "un-American." Yasmin, an African-born wife, said she felt uncomfortable about having a full-time live-in servant, and Randi told me,

> We had a house man, house boy. That was hard to get used to. You know, it sounds great and most people just love having somebody, but I found it a little uncomfortable at first, especially coming from the South. Having this guy, he was calling me master, he was calling my husband master, and stuff like that. It was bizarre.

Cecile told me that she was pressured into hiring a household staff because it was "expected":

> That's another thing I didn't know how to do. Everybody had a nanny, everybody had this and that. So I said, "I don't need all these people." "Oh well, in this country they expect you to do that. You'll see, you'll need them." And so I hired these people and I eventually decided that it wasn't me. It just wasn't me. I couldn't do it. It was okay for me to have someone maybe to do the dishes or do the errands, but my house was my house and I'd always done it all. That was the worst adjustment.... I cannot sit and be served in my own house.

However, several really appreciated having employees to take care of daily chores and assist with the expected representational work.

Two-thirds of these women reported that they had participated in volunteer and women's club activities at post, a slightly lower proportion than for the older wives. Some enjoyed these activities because they were a chance to meet and socialize with people, but others felt that they were pressured into participating. When I asked Sandra if

she had been active with the embassy wives' group at a
particular embassy, she told me,

> Yeah, I was, and the reason was...it was the kind
> of thing that if I didn't do this, I would be viewed
> as not helpful or snobby or something like that.
> And I was almost viewed like that because I was
> a lawyer. I wasn't viewed like that, but I could
> be viewed like that at any minute because I was
> working and I was a lawyer. So I kind of went
> out of my way to go help sew the dumb bun-
> nies. I worked at the bazaar. I did all that stuff.

Note the contrast between Sandra's characterization of
her volunteer activities as "sewing the dumb bunnies" and
the pride with which the older wives spoke about the positive changes their volunteer efforts brought to different
parts of the world.

All of these women know that their participation, or
nonparticipation, is no longer officially evaluated. Yet they
worry about what the community will think of them if
they reject the traditional wives' activities. Many wives are
happy to give of themselves when it is their choice, yet
they resent being pressured to do so. Some stay away from
embassy activities altogether. Sarah even expressed sym-
pathy for the senior wives and told me that she wouldn't
want to be an ambassador's wife herself because the responsibilities are still too great:

> I told my husband, if you don't become ambas-
> sador or DCM that's fine. You're treated like
> the first lady, you're like the little president and
> first lady of that little country. And people are
> so critical of you. I don't know if I could handle
> that.

"The Marriage Bears the Stress"

FIVE OF these twenty-one women have had, or are currently having, serious marital problems that they directly
attribute to their husbands' being in the Foreign Service.

Of those who denied any severe marital difficulty, many mentioned the stresses and problems that come with moving every few years, which most non-Foreign Service couples do not face.

One study of thirty-five couples who moved found that moving can exacerbate troubles that are already present in a marriage.[3] Jacqueline, who has said she will stay home if her husband is posted abroad again, told me that she saves news clippings and articles about the harmful effects of moving on families and children to show to her husband. She says he does not yet believe that she will remain without him, but she is determined not to be uprooted again.

Elizabeth said that she goes into a "ritual year of depression after moving":

> Each time we move takes about a year out of the happiness of my life.... And the marriage is really what bears the stress. Because I try my best not to vent on my children, so I vent on my husband! And of course he has his own stresses, transitional problems and everything, and he vents on me, so it's really tough on the marriage each time we move.

Elizabeth's husband decided to join the Foreign Service after they had been happily married for several years. She has considered divorce more than once, and she and her husband have been in marriage counseling.

Jan was in a similar situation in that her husband, again after several years of being happily married, decided virtually on his own to join the Foreign Service. She told me,

> It finally came to a head, because I couldn't stand it anymore. I felt that my life was moving along with his, but nobody had ever asked me if I wanted to do that. The assumption was just made that of course he's going, so I'll go. And there I was, saying nobody asked me. I resented that nobody asked me what I wanted to do, and I don't necessarily want to do this. And he was

real upset…this was something he really wants
to do, and he really loves it. And so it's a tradeoff. I love him, so therefore I can't ask him not
to do the job that he loves to do…. But then the
thought of going out again just makes me panic.

Jan dislikes moving to foreign countries. A teacher, she
has been able to practice her profession without interrup-
tion, and in spite of her unease, she has thus far decided to
stay with her Foreign Service husband.

In a similar case, a very unhappy wife admitted that
she was unsure if the relationship would survive because
her husband had really already chosen the Foreign Service
over her:

He likes it. He likes what he does. He even admitted and said to me straight out that he knows
it's terrible for me, and he knows I'm miserable, but he's selfish enough, he likes it enough,
and that's what he wants to do. And he's going
to keep on doing it. (Marjorie)

Some men do place their career before their marriage:

I think some men put certain things first. I think
some put career first, some put family first. You
have to make that split. I think very few, some
can, but few can do both well. So in my case I
think it's career. That's fine. (Jacqueline)

Jacqueline seems to have accepted the fact that her
husband's commitment to the Foreign Service precedes
his commitment to her. While she does not want a divorce, she also does not want to go overseas again. Similarly, others say they have had marital troubles because of
the work demands of the Foreign Service. They complain,
as do some of the older wives, that they hardly ever see
their husbands:

He thrives on pressure. His father was a workaholic, that's the only sort of example he had. And

he feels like he has to make himself irreplaceable at his job, or else nobody's going to take him seriously.... And that's the kind of attitude that the Foreign Service takes and runs with.... He sometimes works fourteen, fifteen hours a day.... And sometimes, by the time he gets home, I mean, he walks in the door, he takes off his clothes, and goes to sleep. That's it.... I mean, you know, he doesn't have time for anything, which means that...I have to take care of every-thing, I have to take his suits to the dry cleaner. I have to do his laundry, I have to pack him a lunch in the morning. He calls me up, "Pack me a suitcase, I've got to be on a plane at one o'clock, come and pick me up, take me to the airport." (Marjorie)

Also, as with some of the older wives, couples dis-agree over representational activities. Yasmin, a particu-larly shy young woman, told me that every time they were expected to attend a reception, typically a large gathering, she would pick a fight with her husband and then tell him she was not going. Only over time did she realize that she was unconsciously terrified of attending these affairs and was making up excuses for not going. In this case cer-tainly the demands of the job were negatively affecting the marriage.

Thus, while a minority of these respondents report significant marital difficulties, these serious problems are directly due to the Foreign Service lifestyle. The State De-partment keeps no official statistics on divorce rates for Foreign Service personnel; I was told by one employee that the rate is believed to be lower than in the rest of the population, and another said that the rate is about the same as in the general population. A study of the relation-ship between family pressures caused by professions like the Foreign Service and the divorce rate within such pro-fessions is needed.

One study has found that for wives who move for the sake of their husband's career, whether or not they felt at home in their new place of residence after two years was directly related to whether or not they had involved themselves in work, paid or not.[4] The next chapter describes what career-oriented women have done regarding work.

NOTES

1. There is a perception that male American Foreign Service officers are increasingly marrying foreign-born women, due to "the growing reluctance of potential American partners to live the uprooted lifestyle" [Jewell Fenzi, *Married to the Foreign Service: An Oral History of the American Diplomatic Spouse* (New York: Twayne, 1994), p. 251]. Although I interviewed an equal number of foreign-born wives in each of my two subsamples (two each), my sample is not a representative one, so that from my study, at least, one can draw no conclusions about the percentage of spouses that are foreign-born and whether this has been increasing or not. Considering, however, that there are more single individuals entering the Foreign Service today, one could hypothesize that more officers are meeting their future spouses overseas, since they spend years away from the United States. Because female officers are more likely than male officers to be single, it will be interesting to see whether the numbers of foreign-born Foreign Service husbands will increase in the future.

2. Audrey T. McCollum, *The Trauma of Moving—Psychological Issues for Women* (Newbury Park, CA: Sage Publications, 1990).

3. Ibid.

4. Ibid.

6

Careers, Jobs, and Identities

As DESCRIBED IN THE preceding chapter, the majority of the younger women grew up believing that they would pursue a career. Many of them were already doing so when the Foreign Service entered their lives. At that point, in contrast to the previous generation of wives, who tended not to be very career-oriented, many of the younger wives thought long and hard about how they could, or could not, adapt their career to the Foreign Service lifestyle.

For example, Sarah, a 32-year-old who had an international upbringing and describes herself as a "global person," was concerned that her professional life would be curtailed by becoming a Foreign Service wife. Unfortunately, as she found while working at a large embassy overseas as a spouse employment specialist, many spouses fail to consider the impact of Foreign Service life on their careers. Her mission was to try to make more jobs available to spouses and to assist those who desired employment. She described to me the common situation:

> I don't want to get like so many women that I met when I was working as the personnel specialist, who are doctors and lawyers, or people with Ph.D.s in psychology, and they suddenly come to this foreign country and they can't find work and they're told that all they can do is work in clerical or administrative work in the embassy. I don't ever want to resent my husband for that.

I knew when we got married what I was getting myself into.

Mary, a trained nurse, explained her situation:

> You know, they say, oh, she can get a job wherever you go, well not so, obviously.... And I don't think my husband was aware of that, either, so it was sort of an eye-opener for both of us. And I think he was sensitive to that but yet he had his own job.... I think the hardest thing for me was not having an actual someplace to go everyday, because I had been so used to doing that....

While a professional nurse might assume that her skills would be in demand everywhere, the fact is that some countries do not allow foreigners to take jobs. As noted in Chapter 3, the United States has bilateral work agreements with only sixty-three countries, and some of those countries place restrictions on the type of work family members can pursue. Thus, no matter what one's skills, one is never guaranteed a paying position outside the embassy (called "on the economy").

Those who are aware that possibilities for paid work on the economy are limited look to the government for jobs. The State Department is making an increasing number of overseas embassy and consulate positions available to spouses, as will be described in greater detail below. However, as Jacqueline said,

> The husbands are always saying, well, you can get jobs at the embassy, you can get secretarial jobs at the embassy. Or teaching jobs.... But most of us didn't want that, we wanted to do something else.

What many of these women want is to pursue the occupation of their choice, as they had previously been doing, but they find this to be nearly impossible in the Foreign Service.

Feeling Worthless Without a Career

OF THE twenty-one wives in this group, more than two-thirds have a profession—a specific area in which they are trained and have experience. Four are attorneys, three are teachers, and the rest are in areas such as health care, the fine arts and performing arts, and the nonprofit sector. Many are not currently working in their area of expertise because of their husband's profession, and a few are outright angry about this. For example, I was told,

> I am really mad about my career. It is completely destroyed, completely. Partly, I guess in a way, I could consider it my fault, but it's really because we are in the Foreign Service. Even if I could get back to work easily, which maybe I could, maybe I can't, I don't really know, but it's just lost years of my life, and years of the opportunity to be working full-time or part-time at something interesting. (Sandra)

> I feel like my career has been completely derailed.... I don't see how I will ever be able to do in the conventional sense what I want to do, what I've been trained to do, if my husband keeps on doing this and I stay with him while he's doing this. (Marjorie)

Teaching is frequently mentioned as one profession that is relatively portable, and thus a good one for Foreign Service wives. The three wives who are teachers have always found work overseas, though not always for pay. I asked Jan how she would feel if there were no teaching position available at the next post:

> Oh I don't know. I truly don't know.... I've always worked. It's twenty years now that I've taught school and it's so much a part of me that I don't know. I probably would be extremely unhappy.... You know, my idea of being a Foreign Service wife is teaching, and then doing

my part as a Foreign Service wife, after my family and after my job and that sounds terrible but
there's almost this inner resentment that says,
look, I don't have to be part of this, it's not
high on my list of things to do. But if I didn't
have my job, I probably would make my
husband's life really miserable.

Christine is an attorney, and she and her husband are
seriously thinking about leaving the Foreign Service. She
described the negative psychological effects of temporarily
leaving the world of paid employment:

Part of it is, every time I'm away from the profession I lose my nerve and think, oh God, am I
going to do anything? What am I ever going to
find to do in the real world? Just being away is
hard. You lose your confidence, you really do....
I haven't really done anything real in the Foreign Service. You can make it sound, like the
CLO job, traveling, people are impressed with
it, you can make it sound great. But inside I
know it's not real work, really doing something.
So part of it is thinking, what am I going to do,
am I going to be able to go back and make it
again, like I was?

Sandra also described the loss of confidence she experienced when she left the working world:

I really have lost a lot of confidence. In terms of
looking for jobs, the idea of it just makes me ill.
I just want someone to come and say, work for
me, this is a great job. And I also don't know
what I want to do anymore. And a lot of my
skills I've lost, and all my knowledge I've lost.
So it's really frustrating in that way.

Thus not only do Foreign Service wives lose continuity on
their résumés, they also lose the self-assurance and expertise that is built up over the course of a career. One study
found that career-oriented wives suffered psychologically

when they were forced to accept lesser jobs than they had previously held after moving for the sake of their husband's career.[1]

However, Sandra and Christine said that being in a profession, even if they're not currently gainfully employed, gives them the self-esteem that makes being a Foreign Service wife bearable:

> And on top of it, you see, we were both lawyers, and we had this fallback career, which a lot of people in the Foreign Service don't have.... Where I think a lot of other Foreign Service officers with spouses maybe feel more trapped by not having had a previous career or job. And I sort of felt like, having gone to [an elite] law school, that that was sort of a safety net for me. That in a way, wherever I went, people would know about it, and when I come back, now that I'm supposed to be looking for a job, that supposedly that will help me. I think if I hadn't done that I wouldn't have wanted to join the Foreign Service at all. (Sandra)

> I feel sorry for the new wives going in that have never worked or have just started a profession or don't have a profession. Because having a law degree gives me overseas a legitimacy that—as soon as the ambassador hears that I'm an attorney, it's like I'm a different person, I'm a real person as opposed to just a spouse. (Christine)

Being "just a spouse," at least for these young wives, is not a valued role. Rachel, also an attorney, illustrates the point that these women recognize that in our culture a paid job counts for a great deal:

> I think it would be very hard to spend a long period without working. Financially it's always hard. He makes decent money, but as you know, our lifestyle is more expensive than other people's.... I think for Americans really, a lot of their self-esteem is bound up in what they do.

And I don't think it's that way for other cultures necessarily. And for people to say they're not working, I always feel when someone asks me what I'm doing, and I happen to be unemployed at the time, I just feel so worthless. And that's a tough thing to deal with. When I finally quit my last job that was the big issue, am I going to be able to deal with not working for four months until we leave? It's still an issue. It's easier for me to deal right now with not working, but I'd still rather be working. I'd still rather have some profession or career, and not just say, I'm working here, I'm working there.

For these well-educated women, working "here and there" is not enough to grant them high self-esteem. They need a true career in order not to feel "worthless." One can contrast this with the woman in the last chapter who said she was glad that in her day women could be proud to be just wives and mothers. The younger women expect more of themselves and perceive that society values them more when they are pursuing a profession. Thus the Foreign Service lifestyle and its constraints pose a real difficulty for these women.

Even those who wanted a break from the paid professional world in order to have children and stay home to raise them express ambivalence about their situation. Christine, while glad to be home with her children, still misses her professional identity:

You know, I don't have to work, I'm lucky I can be home with the kids. But when you're used to working and having a professional life...it's very very hard not to. And making money in our culture is part of your identity. It does define you. Doing welfare work or other volunteer stuff just isn't the same, for whatever reason, in our culture.... I'm spending my whole life doing things for other people; not only that, but running chores for other people. They're not my things. You know? It's not my life—I'm taking care of other things, other people.

Christine has convinced herself that being able to stay at home with her children is a luxury that others are unable to have, and for which she should be grateful. Yet she does not define herself as one who takes care of other people; these things are "chores." For these baby-boomer women, being a mother and "wife of" is not a career.

"Underpaid and Underappreciated"

EIGHTEEN OF these twenty-one women held paying jobs overseas at some point. Eight found work at post, four worked on the economy, and six did both at different points. The State Department is aware that spouses want jobs, and it is coming around to seeing that for certain tasks it makes sense to hire spouses, rather than bring in a new officer at greater expense. So-called PIT jobs, for "part-time, intermittent and temporary," are available to spouses at posts abroad. These positions offer notoriously low pay, and many respondents complained about them. For example:

> And I'm willing, as a very, very last resort, I'm willing to work in a PIT job. It's very offensive, what they pay PITs.... I've seen it in ——, the PIT employee is doing the pure consular work, which is really a consular job, who's getting paid less than a junior officer who had no experience. She had experience and he had no experience and he was getting more money than she was.... And you know, I think it's very demoralizing. To say, we want you to do these jobs, but we're going to pay you less than we pay secretaries. So, I just find that really offensive. (Rachel)

Many took such jobs because there were no other alternatives, not because the positions held interest for them. I asked Christine, who had worked in an embassy personnel office, what the job consisted of:

> Personnel assistant. A lot of garbage. I mean, it wasn't stimulating or all that interesting, it was

just to have a job. I wasn't all that happy in it, but you get to the point where you're lucky, or you're made to feel like you're lucky to have anything. At least it was a job.

Similarly, Marjorie, the doctoral candidate, told me,

So I went to work there at the consulate basically to get out of the house.... But, you know, on the whole I was doing things like labeling file folders, Xeroxing articles out of the newspaper (laughs). And the money was awful. The money was just terrible.

It seems, then, that in spite of the low pay such positions offer and the fact that the spouses rarely found the work satisfying, many accepted these jobs for lack of other opportunities.

Another reason for working at these jobs was financial need. Randi, who has a college degree in psychology, told me that she and her husband really needed a second paycheck:

You know, government salaries are not high and —— was not a cheap place to live. And when I wasn't working the first few weeks or months, I found that every time you go out you spend a fortune! And we just couldn't afford it, we needed more money. So I went to the CLO at the embassy and said, "I want a job," and the first thing she said was, "Can you type?" And my heart just sank, I said, "No, I don't type, and I'm not looking for a secretarial job." She said, "That's all there is right now and we're desperate." Well, I went to work.

The secretarial job paid $15,000 a year in 1988. She pointed out how demoralizing it can be if this level of pay is the most one can look forward to:

I was finding, though, it really frustrated me to go from, I guess in our first post I was making

$20,000 or so a year, and that was fine with me.
I thought that was a fine salary, I didn't have a
problem with it, it was a great supplement to my
husband's income. But when we went to our next
post, I was making $15,000 as a secretary. And
that was such a blow to my ego, I really had a
hard time with that. Because I had a college degree, and I had had a job that paid more. And
they're supposed to match your income, but they
wouldn't do it, they said they couldn't pay me
more than they paid the Foreign Service secretaries, especially since I didn't have the skills....
But I found it really hard to work for so much
less. And it started dawning on me that it's going to get harder and harder in the Foreign Service. The first post I thought was great, I have a
good job.... But by the time I got to the second
post...I thought, what about when I'm 40 and
the best I can do is $15,000 a year? I mean, it's
not even worth working to me.

Spouses cannot look forward to their salaries increasing over
the years in a regular way. Besides the low pay, the intermittent nature of the work opportunities is also a drawback. I
asked Rachel, who had had several jobs in a very short period, if she had been happy with any of them:

Well, no. I ended up making like six dollars an
hour and they were not very stimulating. I guess
it's really hard to get used to. As an attorney
you're responsible for everything yourself. You
have lots of responsibility. Working one of those
PIT jobs, you can't do anything without getting
three signatures.... But the hard thing is I think
to keep moving every two or three years, trying
to find another job is really hard. It's really tough
to have some continuity in your résumé. When
you have had fifteen jobs in three years, it doesn't
look very good.

Thus, many wives go from post to post, taking whatever
jobs are available, in spite of low pay and positions that

require little from them intellectually. The poor compensation and the lack of continuity in employment are undesirable in themselves and also work against their chances for future employment.

More desirable, and not a PIT job, is the community liaison officer position. As explained earlier, the Family Liaison Office was created by the Department of State in 1978 to attend specifically to the needs of Foreign Service families. Little by little, individual offices were instituted at every post abroad (with the exception of very small posts), with the job of family liaison officer traditionally going to a wife. The name was changed to community liaison officer (CLO) at a later point so as not to exclude officers without families. Each CLO at post decides what she (or occasionally today, he) believes the community needs most: welcoming activities, morale-boosting, support for children, the organization of American holiday festivities, etc. These positions are typically thirty-nine hours a week, so that the Department of State does not have to pay the benefits that would come with a forty-hour-a-week position. The CLO job is sometimes shared between two women.

Five respondents served as the CLO overseas at least once (one has taken the CLO job three times, at each post where she has been). While these women said that the CLO job pays better and is better respected than the PIT jobs, they still complained about the low salary. A woman who served as full-time CLO in the last few years told me that her salary was $26,000 a year. Amanda, who worked as a CLO, said,

> We were really overworked and underpaid and underappreciated. People had a tendency to come in and complain to you all the time and no one ever said thank you. And I worked extremely long hours that I wasn't paid for. But I did it because I wanted to contribute to the embassy community, and it got me out of the house, and I felt more involved in the community.

As the State Department increasingly realizes that paying jobs will help make spouses happy, it has tried to provide more of them. As discussed in Chapter 3, spouses who have worked abroad in a PIT job for at least a year receive executive order eligibility, which facilitates their applying for positions at the various government agencies upon returning to Washington, D.C. The spouse is already considered to be a government employee and thus is more easily eligible for positions. In addition, the American Family Member Associates (AFMA) program helps spouses get better-paying and more responsible jobs overseas. According to an unclassified Department of State cable, which was distributed to all posts abroad,

> One of the goals of the program is for the Department to develop a more formal relationship with Foreign Service spouses who wish to realize long-term, continuing employment with the U.S. government as they accompany their career employee sponsors on overseas and domestic assignments. At the same time, the AFMA program initiative addresses certain staffing requirements for overseas missions and for the domestic offices of the Foreign Affairs agencies, as well as of other U.S. government agencies. The AFMA program is based on Foreign Service spouses' commitment to U.S. government employment, and management's commitment to provide continuity of employment, to the extent possible through the use of official personnel tracking, increased access to training, leave without pay, and expeditious revalidation of security clearances.[2]

Thus the U.S. government may accomplish two desirable things simultaneously: make spouses happier by hiring them overseas when and where there is a personnel need, and in doing so save money by avoiding sending another officer and his or her family overseas.

Still, I was told of several cases where the government hired special consultants or brought in Foreign Service officers on temporary duty to fill gaps at posts abroad when fully capable and qualified spouses were available to perform those tasks. Department of State officials finally may be recognizing the inefficiency of conducting business in this manner and realizing that hiring spouses can be to everyone's advantage. Yet not every spouse can be eligible for the new programs, and so there are still disgruntled spouses. Sandra told me in a frustrated tone that

> They started this thing that if you worked in a PIT job or a government job for a year, then you could be on this list, and when you come back you can work for the government. Well, I'm not eligible because when I was working in —— I was being paid on a voucher system and I wasn't being paid as a PIT.... So first of all, here I am, I've gone to a prestigious law school, I've worked for years, but I'm not eligible for this program to work for the government. This does not make sense to me. Why do you have to work for a year to be eligible to work? It doesn't make sense.... This subject just makes me so angry. So here I am, I want a job, but I can't be a preferred spouse.... And all the CLO and personnel officers treat it like, well this is such a big advance, now we have this wonderful thing. I guess that's true in a way, but as far as I'm concerned, it's great if you can be in it, but how do you get into it in the first place?

Repeatedly I was told that although State Department officials try to give the impression that they really care about spouses and are making an effort to address their concerns, the situation really has not improved. The much-celebrated skills bank that has been set up by the Family Liaison Office in Washington, the purpose of which is to match spouses with employment, was called "a joke" by Marjorie, who had registered with the skills bank to no effect whatsoever.

Finally, there was the perception that male spouses are luckier when it comes to finding jobs overseas:

> I really feel that the system favors male spouses. There was some evidence of that in ——.... There

was a woman political officer who really knew
the DCM [deputy chief of mission] well, and
when the time came to choose a CLO, she pushed
for her husband to be chosen. And he had only
been there a short time, or only was going to be
there a short time or something, and there was
somebody else who was quite qualified, and they
chose him. And the ambassador was heard to
say... "Of course we had to get him a job because
of course a man needs a job." And that really
bent a lot of people out of shape. (Sandra)

Later in this book I will report on my conversations with
male spouses.

"Always a Dependent"

As WAS true with the older generation of Foreign Service
spouses, half of the younger group question their identity. They said that their identity was changing, or that
they were looking for a new one; and in spite of their original orientation toward careers, only two mentioned their
profession. Four women unhesitatingly described themselves in other ways (such as "I am my name"), and five
identified themselves as mothers, or as primarily family-
oriented.

Kate is an example of one who, at least at this particular time, unequivocally defined herself primarily as a
mother: "I feel like somebody's mom right now. I do feel
like somebody's mom." However, she went on to say, "And
I really want to find something for me right now. And I
don't know what that's going to be yet.... I really need to
find my thing." Kate had also given up her career for a few
years. At the time of our interview she and her husband
had decided mutually that he should leave the Foreign
Service so that their children would have roots in the
United States. After being uprooted by the Foreign Service and spending several years as a full-time mother, it
will take Kate some time to figure out her aspirations.

Several mothers resisted defining themselves as Kate
did. From Lisa I heard:

I don't like being the wife and mother. I don't
like that at all. I remember when we first joined
the Foreign Service and I would meet other
Americans, usually at parties, these women had
multiple degrees and were just at home with the
kids. I would turn them off—what could I have
to say to them? Now, suddenly, this is what
people are thinking of me! I hate it, I hate it....
And here I am in the same position now. So I
like having a job, I like having an identity outside of being a wife and mother.

Sandra, another former career woman, also described the
low opinion she had of housewives before she became one
herself:

It just seems like I've become like what I used
to hate. I remember when I was working as a
lawyer and I went to some partner's house. His
wife was there and I said, "Are you working?"
And she said, "No," and I said, "How do you
spend your time?" I just couldn't fathom her
life. And she said, "Well, I have my kids." And I
couldn't talk to her, I had nothing to talk to her
about. I couldn't understand her life at all. And
I've become her.

Many of these women, including those who identify
themselves as feminists, noted that feminism has been
hostile to women who choose to be housewives and stay-
at-home mothers, or at least has been perceived that way.
They believe that the feminist movement is partially responsible for the denigration of the housewife and mother
role in America. Rachel, an avowed feminist, said,

I think some homemakers feel very threatened
by feminism because it sort of invalidates their
choices. You know, they perceive it that way. And
you don't want to look at that because you may
at some level agree with that, and then you'd
have to be forced to look at yourself and say,

"Gee, I've wasted my time." That's not a thing anybody wants to do.

The contemporary women's movement has come to be perceived as so hostile to traditional women that mothers who stay home with their children are not sure if they can call themselves feminists. Sarah, a very happy mother of a young girl, finds that women are "mean" to each other. She does not identify herself as a feminist because:

> Women have made women feel badly for the choices they make in their lives, that's why. The whole idea of the feminist movement was to give women choices.... And I've been treated badly by female Foreign Service officers because of the choices I've made.... So no, I'm not a feminist. No. I think women have in many ways been their own enemies.

Few of these women wanted to define themselves as their husband's wife. One woman said laughingly that if I had met her a few years ago she would have described herself as a Foreign Service spouse, but in the meantime she has become anti-spouse. Officially, these women are not even spouses in the eyes of the U.S. government— they are "dependents." In the course of the interviews, several talked about how they felt when the government referred to them as dependents. For example:

> That's my official designation, dependent spouse.... That's what you are. I tried—when I first got there I kept my own name—and it just wore me down. People couldn't find me. (Linda)

> I was always a dependent, and that's what's so frustrating. I'm sure you've heard that before, everything's "dependent." Over here I have my own bank account, this and that. You know over there the local bank called up my husband down at the office to make sure his little wife could take out money! (Jacqueline)

Similarly, several complained about how they must always use their husband's social security number instead of their own in any dealings with the government, which makes them feel less like an individual:

> I used to say, when my husband first went into the Service and for a long time thereafter, I had become no more than an appendage to his social security number. It really went down the wrong way with me. When I was at medical I filled out all these forms, and where it said social security number I put my social security number, and then one of the nurses said, "Oh, what's this number?".... And she said, "Oh no, we don't want yours, we want the employee's number." (Marjorie)

Wives who have given up their professional identities, some supposedly only temporarily while they have children, were most at a loss when asked to describe who they are. Elizabeth, who has been unable to pursue her own professional dream because of the constant relocation, responded to my question in this way:

> These days I say, "I'm nobody, who are you?" You know, Emily Dickinson? "I'm nobody, who are you?" That's usually what I say now because that's what I feel like, nobody.

This represents the extreme of feeling invisible and unimportant.

Others weren't quite so negative. As mentioned above, some women find the Foreign Service to offer a welcome break from their careers so that they can raise their children. When I asked one woman about her identity, she said,

> Oh boy. I don't know. I've done some soul-searching about that. And I really feel like I've kind of lost it, I don't really know what it is.

And maybe that's better because I really feel like
you have to be so flexible in the Foreign Service. And for the spouses, maybe even for the
officers, you have to take on a different persona
all the time. There's this one part of me that's
very career-oriented and I worked really hard in
my career, but I was so willing to give it up when
I left, I was just sick of it. I got really burned
out. And now I've taken on this mother role,
but my daughter is getting old enough, she can
go off and do her thing and doesn't have to be
tied to me all the time. So I'm sort of in this
transitional stage I think.... I'm really happy to
be sort of a free spirit right now, I just wonder
how long that will last. (Amanda)

This woman seems to be enjoying the freedom of her "transitional stage" but does not know how long it will satisfy
her or what she will do next. Rachel, who also seems to be
in a transitional stage, said,

I guess you have to really figure out who you
are and what you want, given this lifestyle. I really haven't figured out what I want out of it. I
haven't really given that as much thought as I
should. At first getting into it, I think I was just
reacting to it.... I just really have to think about
what I want to do. If I could figure out something I could get out of this lifestyle independently, that's my major challenge.

French-born Cecile said that the problem is not so
much who she is but where she belongs:

I'd say that's a big problem. Basically I am a wife.
And I think that inside you kind of fight that,
because before, maybe I was a teacher and that
was a big deal to me, you know, I was proud of
it.... But no, the tough question is, where do you
belong? If something happened to my husband,

what would I do? Where would I go? It's all
part of the identity, that I don't belong anywhere.... And what do I tell my kids? Where do
they belong?

This theme of insecurity is a recurring one. When financial
stability, status, and even a sense of belonging are all derived
from one's spouse, one's position can be precarious.

Twenty-seven-year-old Yasmin was discovering that
the initial satisfaction she felt in just being a wife was beginning to wane; she told me that she wanted to find a job
so that she could introduce herself to others in the context of her own work instead of always describing herself
as her husband's wife. And Beth, who has been to only
one post with her husband, and who had thought long
and hard before deciding to marry a Foreign Service officer, told me that it was very difficult for her to accept her
new identity as "Foreign Service wife," especially because
she felt she hadn't really chosen it.

The topic of identity brought out a generational rift.
Rachel said,

You know, certainly it's a role that I find really
offensive, the "spouse," and you're really looking at female spouses, you're not putting the
same things on male spouses. I just find it offensive. And I also do think there's a certain generational problem too that I'm sensitive to, the
fact that these women who've been doing this
for twenty years, they can easily be offended by
my attitude. I try and not say, "You made the
wrong choice." They're probably thinking,
"Gee, if I had this to do over again, I certainly
wouldn't." I think now is still a groundbreaking
time. The system can't continue to get more
and more women who are willing to do these
kinds of things.... But you know, people make
the best out of their options. The older generation who really did all these things and did them
well, made the most of their choices, you know?
Which is something that should be positive. But

you know, if they had other choices they might
not have chosen that.

Rachel, 38 and highly educated, represents the extreme of
the newer generation of Foreign Service wives who label
the traditional spouse role and expectations of its performance "offensive." Yet she understands how her attitude
can be seen as insulting to those women, past and present,
who have embraced the role. Again, it is an issue of choice,
and from the previous chapter it is clear that the older
generation did make the most of their choices; they do
feel generally happy about how they lived their lives. These
younger wives are definitely struggling more than their
older counterparts over whether to accept or resist the
"spouse" role; they are unsure of their identities and how
to feel satisfied with their choice of husband and lifestyle,
a choice that has restricted subsequent choices.

Uncommitted Wives

As THE preceding comments indicate, the younger group
of wives express more general dissatisfaction than the
older group. Of the twenty-one discussed in this chapter, Elizabeth, Jan, and Marjorie are quite miserable as
Foreign Service wives, but they don't want divorces and
their husbands won't leave the Service; Kate, Christine,
and Sandra are engaged in discussions with their husbands about leaving the Foreign Service; and Jacqueline
has decided she will not go overseas again with her husband but does not want a divorce. Thus one-third of this
sample are clearly dissatisfied with this lifestyle. And what
is most important for at least half of these younger respondents is whether or not they can find interesting work
at a post.
    Yet their unhappiness is not entirely due to the in-
ability to pursue their careers; in more than one case the
main factor is that the wife detests moving and does not
wish to live outside of the United States. For those who
do not wish to live abroad, it makes no difference whether
the post is a place like Belgium, where living conditions
are comfortable, or Nigeria, where life is more arduous.

The younger women did tend to describe more posts in negative terms than did the older wives, but this may be because the younger wives' experiences are more recent and time has not yet caused the most difficult moments to fade. Respondents remarked that some posts were particularly challenging because of terrorist threats (Ann), conservative, restrictive practices toward women (Rachel), and a great deal of crime (Teresa), to give a few examples. Yet the women did not hold the Foreign Service in general responsible for the problems of these particular places. "I was inclined to say to myself, it's just this post," Teresa said; "The country's the country. Every country's different," said Kim. As Randi said, with great pleasure and pride in her voice, "We've been to places nobody has ever heard of. I wouldn't trade those experiences for anything."

Of the two-thirds who are satisfied for the time being, two are successful in portable careers. They also generally enjoy Foreign Service life. Four say that the Foreign Service fulfills their most important desire at present: living overseas. Three others assert that the Foreign Service provides a way for them to stay home to raise their children, so that the lifestyle suits them for now. The last five respondents from this group say that the Foreign Service is fine for now, and "we'll see."

The unhappiest women are the three whose husbands made a unilateral decision to join the Foreign Service. For example, Elizabeth, a very talented woman who was not able to fulfill her career dreams, said,

> A source of great pain is to think my life has been wasted. You know, it may be hubris on my part to think that I was especially gifted. But I do think that (laughs). And thinking that I have this gift and that it never really came to full fruition makes me feel really terrible. I don't know how else to say it. Angry and sad and all those things.... [I asked, "Would you have made a different decision if you knew what you know now?"] Yes. When he came to me and said, "I know what I want to do with my life," I would

have said, "Think of something else" (laughs).
But we were ignorant, what did I know?

Elizabeth recognizes that when her husband joined the
Foreign Service she did not adequately consider how much
his career choice would affect her life and career goals.
She believes the State Department should be more forth-
coming about this:

> Anybody who's a spouse of a Foreign Service of-
> ficer cannot really entertain career ambitions for
> their own self. Just can't.... And they should tell
> people that, when they're taking the test.... ["Like
> a warning label on the exam?" I asked] Exactly!
> "Does your spouse like not working?"'I mean,
> you don't know when you're 20 what's going to
> be important to you when you're 40. You think
> you do, but you change. You do change. And...in
> my case, we were newlyweds, and I was happily
> and madly in love and everything, and just wanted
> whatever he wanted, wanted him to be happy,
> right? When you're in that stage, you don't count
> the cost....

Elizabeth will most likely stay with her husband; she feels
that it is already too late for her to resume her career track.
   One couple is leaving the Foreign Service because of
concerns for their children's health and safety:

> We would have gone overseas in a heartbeat if
> we didn't have kids. Your perspective really
> changes a lot. And maybe we're just not real
> true Foreign Service people. You know, there
> are people who take their kids to India. They
> take their kids to pretty bad places. I wouldn't
> do that. I don't want to force my kids to be
> exposed to diseases that they'll have to carry for
> the rest of their lives. That was our decision....
> If they're older and we decide we want to go
> back out again we can all sit down as a family

and make that decision, then that's what we'll
do. But we just didn't want to impose it on
them. (Kate)

In deciding not to go overseas with her husband again,
Jacqueline also brought up her concerns for her children:

> To think that the Foreign Service is somehow
> splitting up families when that's not the aim, it
> is sad, but there's no trend to stop that from
> happening. So I don't know how it can
> change.... In fact there were some studies, did
> you read that about moving? Saying that they
> had never done research on whether moving is
> really hard on children, they've always looked
> at it from the beneficial angle, how it stimulates
> them. But they've come out and said that it's
> really far more harmful than they ever thought
> on children.

She is not going overseas again, she said, because:

> I have everything I need here, the children are
> happy, my family's happy. I adore traveling, let
> me travel for two or three weeks, but not for
> three years. I feel like it will be three years of
> wasted time. Wasted in the sense of life here is
> just passing me by. I've got two parents with
> cancer, just the thought of going abroad and
> missing those times.... I can't do that.

However, Jacqueline plans to stay married. "Commuter
couples" have become increasingly common as growing
numbers of spouses and children remain in the United
States when the employee is sent overseas.

Not every wife is as tolerant of her husband's career;
for example, Sandra wishes that her husband would leave
the Foreign Service:

> I think it was really a great experience to live
> overseas. But now my kids are older I really want
> to get back to work, they don't really need me

full-time at home. And the idea of moving back overseas again, someplace where I cannot work, is just.... You know, what if we go somewhere with one street and a gas station, I mean, I'd just go out of my mind. They'd have to institutionalize me.... I mean, I'm practically crazy already (laughs).

Sandra also told me,

I've sort of taken my own personal little surveys of successful Foreign Service officers and what their wives do, and the huge majority are either nurses, teachers, or librarians, which are all portable, or they're even more portable like writers and artists and jewelers. Or they're foreign wives who don't want to work, or regular American wives who don't want to work. And there are almost no professionals in the lot.

Barbara, a teacher who would probably balk at being referred to as a nonprofessional, lends support to that statement by saying,

I've never felt restricted or confined or anything like that—I know some people do, some people find it very stifling. But where I've been, and the things I've been able to do, I've so far found it very interesting. I've not regretted wherever we were living, and I haven't been one to count the days.

As the older generation observed, the young wives are not committed to Foreign Service life. I found a great deal of evidence for this. For example:

I don't know if we'll stay in this, I can't say we're committed to it as a long-term career.... (Amanda)

So I do think there's a different mindset, a different attitude of people coming in. But at the time we came in, which wasn't all that long ago,

there was still a question of coming into the Foreign Service as a career. We were not. It was
clear in our minds that we would not do this
forever. (Kate)

Most of the Foreign Service officers that we
know that have left since we started have left
because their spouses have been unhappy.
Women aren't willing to just go to tea parties
anymore. I won't be, either, once my children
are older. (Sarah)

This lack of commitment to the Foreign Service as a life-
long profession is the basic difference between women of
the older generation and those of the newer. Elaine, one
of the younger wives of the older generation, said about
the new wives:

The Foreign Service has changed a lot in the
twenty years we've been in it, and not for the
better.... I just see so many officers and their
families who seem to not want to be overseas,
who want to go and create a little America overseas, they want everything done for them...and
there are fewer families who are feeling committed to being abroad. Everybody's sort of out
for themselves and that's a disquieting thing to
watch happening. It's very hard to gather people
into a community if you feel that way....

Yet while the older generation sees a lack of commitment, the younger believes that the Foreign Service itself
is to blame for their "we'll see" attitude:

If the wife is happy, if the mother's happy, your
children will be happy, too.... The Foreign Service has not taken this into account. I mean,
they make it miserable for the officers, and
they're making it doubly miserable on the family. You know, women leaving their jobs, and
oftentimes their families. I could no more go
somewhere and leave my children in a boarding

school than die. And yet they do that if the husband is assigned to a hardship post. (Jacqueline)

> If I could tell you what I felt an overall theme would be about Foreign Service life.... I think there's a certain overall frustration of Foreign Service wives and always having to put their lives on hold or play second fiddle. And I think that it's going to make some real major changes in the Foreign Service. And they're starting to recognize this, although they're kind of behind the times a little bit and they have to do more, because the single-career family is gone, basically, and to ask spouses, not just wives, but husbands, too, to pick up and leave everything behind, especially career-wise.... (Amanda)

These sentiments were echoed by another wife:

> I think the Foreign Service is going to have to do more. I mean, even with tighter times. I think that what's going to end up happening is there'll just be more people going in for shorter terms.... I don't know how many younger women, a lot of them are going to be professional and educated, are going to be willing to do it for that many years. (Christine)

Mary, the nurse who has enjoyed living overseas but has not always found work while abroad, angrily emphasized the point that while State Department officials seem to be making an effort on behalf of spouses and families, little has changed:

> They don't have the money, nor do they want to allot the money, to support families overseas, nor to encourage families to go overseas.... But it seems like they are, because you have all these programs, you've got OBC and you've got the CLO office.... But the bigger issues they don't address. And when you sit back and realize that you've spent fifteen years of your life in the Foreign Service as

a dependent spouse and that if something happened, let's say you and your husband split, or he
died, or whatever, that whatever benefits you have
go with the husband.[3] The family is not really a
part of the State Department.... [I asked about
the rule on benefits in case of divorce.] That rule
says that I get half of your retirement, unless of
course I marry before I'm 55. And then you get
to decide whether I keep it or not. So, it's not
really mine, is it? You still have all the powers. The
power rests with the employee.... But you are asking families to give up just about everything. You're
asking wives to give up a job, and...I don't believe
a lot of people work because they want a career, I
think they work right now out of necessity.... And
when you go overseas you don't have all the benefits you used to have. It costs money. Every time
we move, we are out of pocket thousands of dollars.... But I think the part that makes me angry is
that they keep pretending that they're doing something about it, and they don't. They have no interest in it at all.

One can see from these words the bitter feelings Mary has
toward "Mother State," as the Department of State is often called. If these feelings are representative of even half
of the younger Foreign Service spouses, and I believe they
are, then the Foreign Service is in trouble.

Conclusion: How Personal Expectations
Clash with the Available Options

IT is not surprising that the older Foreign Service wives I
studied are happier and more satisfied with their lives than
those of the younger generation. Much of this has to do
with what women are brought up to expect for their lives,
and the cultural demands that shape their perceptions of
how women of a certain social position should conduct
their lives. Of course the two—personal expectations and
cultural demands, or biography and history—are related.
Women who grew up before the Second Wave of feminism did not necessarily expect to have professional lives

of their own, while women who grew up during and after the Second Wave know they have that choice. Older women who spent their lives raising their children are not looked down upon in our society; it is recognized that in their time options outside the home were limited for women. On the other hand, college-educated women today who choose to be "only" mothers and wives are disparaged by some in our society. (Some are fighting back, as is shown in this book.) This is partially blamed on the feminist movement, which emphasized one "true" way for the liberated woman instead of free choice for all women.

Thirty-three-year-old Lisa, a mother of two children, remarked on the women's movement and generational differences between women:

> Sometimes I think I'm really glad about the women's movement, but sometimes I think of before the women's movement, I think of my mother, they really didn't have another option, but maybe they were happier that way. It sounds horrible to say, because obviously they weren't, but you know, I just feel like, oh God, there's so much more I would rather be doing, when in fact, that was their lot in life at the time.

Lisa speculates correctly that the wives who came before her, who did not have to relinquish career opportunities because of the Foreign Service, were happier.

Sociologist Kathleen Gerson's work on how women make decisions about their lives emphasizes that women are actors; they "construct their lives out of the available raw materials,"[4] taking into account childhood experiences (biography) and structural constraints (society and history). This is the "choice within constraint" model of human behavior. The women I studied had goals for themselves, and certain ideas of how their lives would turn out. They weren't always able to follow the path they had set for themselves; as they grew up, they had to choose from among the available options. Often, one choice then determined other choices. For example, Linda, who had never decided on any particular career, told me that she had at least always pictured herself as being independent:

Before, I didn't have great career aspirations, so
I can't say I was really giving anything up. But I
always thought I would be self-supporting and
independent. Even when I was thinking about
not working to raise the children, I hadn't quite
seen myself in this dependent role. You don't.
You can't imagine it if you grew up always thinking you would be independent. And I also didn't
quite understand what the Foreign Service was
all about.

Gerson writes that women face "structural ambiguity" when they are faced with imperfect alternatives. "Structural ambiguity," Gerson says, "refers to the uncertainties
within and contradictions between the various work and
family structures women confront."[5] As Foreign Service
wives, the women in this chapter are given a derived, ambiguous role, and are often faced with unwilling unemployment when they have been brought up to expect
professional and financial independence. While they could
choose to leave their mates for geographic stability and
professional fulfillment, that is only another imperfect alternative.

Gerson argues that women of more recent generations face more structural ambiguity, and my study of these
Foreign Service wives supports this claim. This is because
women of more recent generations do have more choices
than women of previous ones. A greater range of choices,
combined with persistent views and institutions that support traditional gender roles, seems to bring about greater
structural ambiguity. The resulting contradictions and
uncertainties promote "not only psychological ambivalence
within individuals and social conflict between opposing
social groups, but also creative individual and social responses."[6] In other words, as women come into contact
with those "damned if you do, damned if you don't" situations, they must create their own strategies of adjustment.
These strategies are either reactive or revolutionary: they
either act to preserve traditional sex roles and relations, or
they act as a force for change.

Foreign Service wives have acted as a force for change;
they fought for, and won, rights for themselves and freedom from obvious abuses. It may be that now, however,

increasing numbers of wives (and husbands) are deciding that they cannot adjust, they cannot be a full individual in an outdated role, so instead of making a full commitment to the Foreign Service, they leave it (and/or their spouses) to follow other paths. As one wife speculated, those who remain will consist of a self-selected group of women with portable careers such as teaching and art, and traditional women who define themselves as wives and mothers. But among my younger respondents, there were very few of the latter.

In the next chapter, we will see that forces for change include a growing number of male Foreign Service spouses and tandem couples. In addition, to present the larger issue of work and family policy, I will address how corporations are contending with some of the same problems I have described. Given the wide range of choices American women now have, and an increasing number of dual-career couples, in the private sector, too, fewer wives are opting to follow husbands to assignments that require a major move. Thus, all kinds of modern-day couples are facing structural ambiguity.

NOTES

1. Naomi Gerstel and Harriet Gross, *Commuter Marriage: A Study of Work and Family* (New York: Guilford Press), 1984.

2. Cable titled "Open Season for the American Family Member Associates (AFMA) Program," February 10, 1993. Since this book went to press, the Family Member Appointment program was launched. This program will attach some government benefits to some PIT positions. The details are still being worked out.

3. The current policy on divorced spouses is as follows: a spouse is entitled to some portion of the employee's pension if they were married for at least ten years, and if the spouse does not remarry prior to the age of 55. The employee's annuity is reduced by the amount that is paid to the spouse. See Department of State Publication 9914, *The Foreign Service Family and Divorce* (1992).

4. Kathleen Gerson, *Hard Choices: How Women Decide about Work, Career, and Motherhood* (Berkeley: University of California Press, 1985), p. 37.

5. Ibid., p. 124.

6. Ibid.

7

Male Spouses, Tandems, and the Corporate Parallel

As SHOWN IN THE previous chapters, employment in the United States Foreign Service affects one's family and spouse to a degree that employment in few other occupations does. Foreign Service wives have been expected to play a role in support of their husband's profession, and even if this expectation is in decline today, wives still follow their husbands around the globe, often forsaking their own careers. The modern twist to this story is that the number of female Foreign Service officers is increasing, which means that more men are becoming Foreign Service spouses. This chapter looks at the interesting situation of the male spouse as well as the growing numbers of tandem couples—those in which both partners are Foreign Service employees.

Although the case of the Foreign Service spouse is extreme, parallels can be drawn with spouses in the private business sector. Due to increasing numbers of dual-career couples, corporations are confronting greater difficulty in transferring their employees freely, as spouses balk at geographic moves that may disrupt their own careers. Hence this chapter also looks to the corporate sector for solutions that may be helpful for the Foreign Service.

Male Spouses: The Newest "Dependents"

APPROXIMATELY 10 PERCENT of Foreign Service spouses are husbands. While the number of male spouses is increasing, incoming female spouses still outnumber incoming male spouses. For example, in a recent entry class of Foreign Service officers, eighteen of the total of thirty-nine junior officers were married, yet of those eighteen, only five were women with male spouses who would be accompanying them as dependents. Four others were women whose husbands were already Foreign Service officers.

While it is unlikely that male spouses will become as commonplace as female spouses anytime soon, greater attention is being paid to the male spouse. In 1989, the results of a survey of male spouses sponsored by the Foreign Service Institute's Overseas Briefing Center were published. Titled *Report on the Role of the Male Spouse in the Foreign Service*, the survey summary was written by Dick Buckley, a Foreign Service consultant and male spouse himself. This report has never been widely publicized or distributed.

Buckley views his report as a "sequel" to the 1985 American Association of Foreign Service Women (AAFSW) report, *The Role of the Spouse in the Foreign Service*. Because women have made up the vast majority of Foreign Service spouses, that report concentrated on wives. The main point of Buckley's report is that there are great similarities "in perceptions and comments among female and male spouses—especially their concerns about the need for better recognition of the contributions they have to make, meaningful employment opportunities, and adequate training."[1]

For the survey, questionnaires were sent to approximately 480 male spouses of Department of State employees in early 1988. Questionnaires were also sent to 65 male spouses of U.S. Information Agency employees. Names and addresses were not available for male spouses of the U.S. Agency for International Development employees, so word of mouth was relied on to inform those spouses about the study and the desire for their participation. By June 1, 1988, 221 questionnaires had been returned, or 41 percent of the total mailed to specific individuals.

The respondents to this survey are well-educated: 71 percent have bachelor's degrees or higher. The range in ages is quite broad, with 59 percent being 25 to 44 years old and the rest being 45 or older. The men come from many different professions and occupations. The demographic information shows that these men represent a new Foreign Service trend: 71 percent have accompanied their wives overseas for four years or less. Thus the vast majority are relatively new to the Foreign Service.

The male spouses who responded to this survey echo their female counterparts in desiring more and better work opportunities overseas. They say that their experience and talents are being wasted and that they would like to see the U.S. government take a more systematic approach to hiring spouses. However, one male spouse's comments repeated an impression that some wives have:

> I also think it's a lot easier for males to get employment. People feel it's a man's place to be employed. Somehow they feel it's not so bad if a woman stays at home, quietly climbing the walls.[2]

Also in accord with the comments of wives, the husbands complained about the low salaries of U.S. government jobs at posts overseas, and a general attitude that they should be glad if they find a paying position at all.

I interviewed three male spouses, one each in his thirties, forties, and fifties. While these three were not randomly selected from the population of male spouses, from anecdotal information I believe that they represent quite well the range of male spouses in the Foreign Service, especially in terms of age, education, employment status, and current satisfaction with their position as dependent male spouses. All three are highly educated; two have doctoral degrees and the third has a law degree. Two have been to two posts with their wives, the other to three. All of these men have found employment while their wives were posted abroad, for example, with international schools, as consultants for AID, and at the embassies. Two of these men served as community liaison officers at embassies overseas, probably among the first male spouses to do so.

The three men represent different life stages in terms of careers. The youngest one, Michael, plans to continue with his career as a consultant. At the time of the interview, Michael was part of a commuter couple; he was working in a State Department position in Washington, D.C., while his wife and child were overseas. He told me that he did not want to be separated from his family again, and that in the future he and his Foreign Service officer wife planned to "take turns" pursuing their careers. He explained that once she receives tenure in the Foreign Service she will be able to take leave without pay occasionally, so they will alternately follow each other.

The middle-aged man, Alexander, wants his wife to retire from the Foreign Service so that he may pick up a career he has put on hold for eight years. This spouse is currently searching for a professional job and in our interview sounded bitter about his prospects. I asked him how he answers when people ask him what he does:

> Well, I tell them that I'm job-hunting. That I'm unemployed and that I'm paying the price for having taken this almost eight-year sabbatical with my wife, and for having served as a sort of Peace Corps volunteer for the American tax-payer, with the difference that I didn't get any type of recognition from the government.... And one of the frustrating things sometimes is that the organizations that you think are there to support you, like FLO [the Family Liaison Office], the Foreign Service Institute, and the Overseas Briefing Center, are controlled by tight-knit cliques that have a very limited understanding of the problems of Foreign Service spouses, professional Foreign Service spouses, returning from overseas after eight or ten years, when they need special help to go back into their career tracks.... And the institutions are not designed for that.... There's limited help.

Consistent with the views of the newer wives, Alexander contends that while Department of State personnel claim to be taking steps to assist spouses, the facilities that are in place are actually not up to the task.

The oldest husband, Edward, had already had a fulfilling career before his wife entered the Foreign Service a little over ten years ago. He does not consider himself retired and has been enjoying himself thoroughly overseas, picking up jobs as he wishes, and performing some consulting work for the Department of State when in Washington.

My research revealed that wives' satisfaction with Foreign Service life often depends on what stage of their life they are in; for example, the Foreign Service suits women who are bearing and raising children. For men also, time of life affects their feelings about the Service; those who are retired or near retirement appreciate the Foreign Service the most. Many husbands, after ending their own careers, are content with a life of foreign travel in their later years.

Regarding the male spouse and representational work, I asked Michael if while overseas he had had to attend any representational functions:

> Did I *have to? Have to* is an interesting word.
>
> [I said, "Wives often feel they *have to.*"]
>
> Yeah, well, that's why it's an interesting word. I think it's a self-imposed *have to*, maybe subtly imposed by external sources, but they're certainly not *required to*. And I often opted not to go, if I didn't want to go. But I also opted to go, even if I didn't want to go. Actually from the sociological perspective, it's fairly interesting sometimes, these cocktail parties!

None of these three husbands complained about representational activities. They are not burdened with the actual labor of entertaining as many of the wives are. Moreover, male spouses generally do not have the same sense as their female counterparts of wanting to support their spouse's career.

More typically, male spouses feel socially out of place; they are treated as deviants by others. The three I spoke with all said that they were often mistaken for the Foreign Service officer and their wife for the spouse. I asked them how they handled this situation and how they described themselves to others at social affairs. Alexander said,

> Well, I would say that I was an international gypsy, or that I was a Foreign Service spouse. And that I had been teaching many years at a university,

and I had decided to go with my wife overseas because I valued the family link, that had a priority in my life, rather than be separated. But many people felt that that expressed very bad judgment on my part, that I had made a very stupid mistake. People, even some U.S. government officials, did not understand that. "What the hell is a guy who's a Ph.D. doing accompanying his wife? He doesn't belong. There must be something behind that." They didn't understand that.... And that is one of the reasons I don't want to go overseas again, because okay, enough is enough.

Edward said,

The men didn't know how to deal with me, the officers. You know, you go to the party, and right away they say, "Gee, I haven't noticed you around, what section are you in?" As soon as you tell them, they might ask one more question and then they're out. Because they don't really know how to go into any other areas, like "What do you do? What's your interest?" That's too scary. So that was difficult for them.

The comments of these two men demonstrate that the male spouse is still an anomaly at Foreign Service posts abroad. It was clearly indicated to them that they were breaking social norms by following their wife and her career.

Buckley's study addressed this problem, reporting that male spouses "perceive that people do not readily accept men who are not in dominant career roles and that they, as men, are usually not requested for volunteer roles."[3] Michael complained about the clubs overseas that are still called "wives' clubs" or "women's clubs"; he stated that such nomenclature was exclusionary and that these clubs should be open to all and renamed "spouse clubs" or "American charitable organizations." As a result of the perception that husbands are not welcome in these associations, male spouses have begun forming their own support groups at some posts. Edward said,

I think one thing we have to start doing is forming male support groups. We did in one post,
because some of the male spouses became very
isolated.... You have to draw them out and help
them find what they can do. And they're usually my age, they're retired themselves, and it's
not easy for them to get out and start interact-
ing with the younger group. So that's one thing,
we started a little support network among the
few male spouses at post.

In summary, it does appear that the male spouses'
concerns are very similar to those of the female spouses.
Consider that the following statement by Alexander could
easily be spoken by a female spouse:

I think that there are some structural adjust-
ments that the U.S. government should make,
to take better advantage of all this wasted talent
that they have in all these embassies, consulates,
and missions overseas. They have a lot of highly
qualified professional people, with tremendous
linguistic skills and professional knowledge, from
the best universities in the world, that are being
underemployed and underutilized. And there
is resentment beginning to accumulate. Of
course, in the case of young spouses of recently
married couples under thirty with babies, that's
a different story. But there are a lot of people
that are over age 30 and that have kids in high
school or in college, and that wasted talent
should be fully utilized.

Of Buckley's respondents, a third said that their frus-
trations as spouses were having an adverse effect on their
wives' satisfaction with their careers. Of the three male
spouses I interviewed, only Edward is perfectly satisfied with
his current lifestyle, and Alexander is pressuring his wife to
retire from the Foreign Service so that he can take up his
own career again. Thus, while the male spouses do not have
representational and volunteer responsibilities, they experience many of the same career difficulties as the female

spouses, along with their own particular problem of an aberrant status as dependent *male* spouses.

With the Department of State intent on recruiting and retaining more female Foreign Service officers, it must address the problems of male spouses. As stated earlier, female Foreign Service officers are much more likely to be single than their male counterparts (this is true for every rank, but it is also true that female Foreign Service officers are currently concentrated in the lower ranks). It is possible that any difficulties the State Department is having in recruiting and retaining women officers are due to the reluctance of husbands (or potential husbands) to become dependent spouses.

Tandem Couples

IN FOREIGN SERVICE parlance, a tandem couple is one in which both members of the couple are Foreign Service employees. It may appear that tandem couples are the ideal "solution" to the spouse problem since both members of the couple can have a full-time career. Yet tandems face their own problems, most notably that each member of the couple must agree, as must all Foreign Service members, to be assigned wherever needed. This means that the State Department can assign members of tandem couples to different posts. While the decision-makers do try to keep couples together as much as possible, couples are not infrequently asked to separate.

A *New York Times* report on tandem couples in the Foreign Service in 1985 found that there were 308 such couples, which constituted 8 percent of the Foreign Service work force and a 6 percent increase over 1984.[4] The article also noted a Foreign Service survey of tandem couples that found that 233 of these couples were assigned together, 25 were assigned to different posts, and in 14 cases one spouse took leave without pay to remain with the other spouse during his or her assignment. Thus the vast majority of the couples surveyed were able to share a household. Taking leave without pay, however, is perceived as harmful to the career of the spouse who makes that choice. Fairness is another issue that frequently arises: when efforts are made to keep tandem couples together, they may cause other deserving officers to be "bumped" from positions at particularly sought-after posts.

Assigning couples to the same post becomes more difficult as the couple becomes more senior, as officers are not allowed to supervise their spouses, and adequate positions for both officers may not be found at one post. The *New York Times* article tells of the situation of one particularly high-level tandem couple: the wife was appointed ambassador to Bangladesh at the same time the husband was appointed ambassador to Nepal. The two ambassadors commuted for three years. Thus it is possible that an increasing number of tandems will contribute to a growing number of commuter couples, which is considered a negative trend.

In spite of the difficulties, the number of tandem couples is increasing. In 1989 there were 317 of these couples; in 1994 there were 382.[5] Tandem couples with whom I spoke were mostly negative about their situation. In one case the couple was considering leaving the Foreign Service, and in another case the wife had joined the Foreign Service after her husband had and only because she had so detested being a Foreign Service spouse. This wife said that they would rather leave the Foreign Service than have to take separate assignments. In general, it seems that tandem couples evaluate their situation one post at a time, with the option of leaving the Foreign Service always a possibility. Tandem couples, then, are perhaps part of the new "uncommitted" era of Foreign Service families.

The Spouse Problem in Corporations

THE SITUATION of some corporate spouses is parallel to that of Foreign Service spouses. Chapter 2 reported on some of the early sociological research conducted on corporate wives. Sociologist William Whyte found that the corporate wives of the 1950s were generally happy with their situation and played their role with ease. In 1977, organizations expert Rosabeth Moss Kanter recognized the importance of addressing spouse issues in corporations:

> How to understand and take into account the
> position of wives is an intellectual task with

relevance for both organizational theory and organizational policy.[6]

Kanter broke with the literature on wives that had described them as willing casualties and analyzed their role in terms of their and the corporation's adjustment to each other. She pointed out that

> The behavior of wives...must be seen in the way we are viewing the behavior of all corporate workers: as a function of their location in the system, as a response to the role constraints within which they operate....[7]

Just as everyone else, wives have choices only within constraints, and thus their actions must be viewed in some sense as reactions. Kanter wrote that perhaps the dilemma of the corporate wife, being both an "insider" and an "outsider," would diminish because the numbers of women willing to fit into the mold "corporate wife" would diminish. She thus foresaw that increasing numbers of women would desire their own independent domain, their own work, and a separate identity.

Yet dilemmas remain. What is still relevant is the issue of geographic relocation. Just as Foreign Service wives resent relinquishing their careers for their husbands', so do corporate wives whose husbands are transferred abroad. This is a significant issue, both for the individuals involved and from the corporate point of view. As in the Foreign Service, as spouses have become less willing to sacrifice their careers for their mates, one result is that the number of global commuter marriages has increased. Instead of one following the other, each member of the couple follows his or her own career path, maintains a separate residence, and commutes to visit the other. Yet dividing families is no answer; one relocation consultant says he finds a 90 percent divorce rate among global commuter couples.[8] Most corporations have informal policies to discourage commuting, and question the commitment of employees whose families don't relocate.[9] When wives do accompany their husbands, companies find that more foreign transfer failures are caused by the poor adjustment of the family than by the employee's work performance, and failed overseas assignments cost companies billions of dollars each year.[10]

As business has become more global, the issue of dual-career couples and the challenge of corporate relocations have become frequent topics in the press. One writer noted that "41 percent of employees transferred abroad have spouses who worked before relocating.... At the same time, global-minded companies are expanding in areas such as Eastern Europe and the Middle East, where spouses of expatriates face particularly tough obstacles to finding jobs."[11] One study found that 42 percent of companies surveyed said that candidates have turned down international positions because of dual-career issues.[12] In response to this problem, more companies are using cross-cultural training programs to try to help the employee and his or her family prepare for moves abroad.

As more companies are challenged by finding employees to send overseas, they are attempting to address the underlying reasons. Increasing numbers of companies are offering spouses assistance in finding employment abroad. For example, some companies provide career counseling, network with other companies to try to locate a job for the spouse overseas, or even hire the spouse themselves. Consulting firms specializing in relocation management are now being employed to assist in these tasks.

Windham International, one such consulting company, "was created by a group of experienced relocation and international human resources professionals to provide expatriate relocation management services to global companies and their employees being sent on international assignments," according to its brochure. The firm performs such services as finding homes in the new location, taking care of moving arrangements, providing health information, educating about cross-cultural issues, and assisting with such things as getting drivers' licenses and bank accounts in the new place of residence. These services are similar to those performed by the government for Foreign Service families.

In 1992, Windham International, in conjunction with the National Foreign Trade Council, conducted a survey to study the impact of family relocation issues on multinational corporations' ability to place employees abroad. Human resources professionals from over 100 companies responded, with two-thirds saying that spouses are a corporate concern and one-third saying that they were not but should be. So the "spouse problem" is significant in corporations.

While the study reports that "most companies feel that spouse careers have a major impact on the rejection of international assignments,"[13] the respondents related little difficulty in filling international positions at the time, and 66 percent said that spousal employment issues have no impact on overseas transfer failure rates. ("Failure" means that transferred employees perform less well than expected or return early to the United States.) One way companies try to avoid spouse-related transfer failure is by sending more single and divorced people overseas, as well as more "traditional families." While most expatriates are married and have children, "some respondents said that more single people are offered or accept international assignments, eliminating the need for addressing the dual-career spouse needs."[14] However, as in the Foreign Service, spouses and families are seen as contributing to a community overseas, which boosts employee morale, and "current literature on the subject suggests that most successful expatriate assignments are married couples with children and that the intact support group helps them to be productive more quickly than single people, who often feel isolated and lonely."[15]

The most important finding of the 1992 survey is that 88 percent of the respondents feel that relocation problems caused by dual-career couples will become more severe. The effects of current demographics are recognized: the proportion of married women employed or seeking work in the United States grew from 51 percent in 1981 to more than 58 percent in 1991, while during the same period the proportion of managers who are women grew from 27 percent to 41 percent.[16] Thus increasing numbers of wives of male employees will be working outside the home or desiring such work, while at the same time, because transferees are usually drawn from management levels, more and more female employees will be given the opportunity to relocate overseas themselves, creating greater numbers of male spouses who will become a concern, as in the Foreign Service.

While, as noted above, two-thirds of the companies reported that spouses were of concern to them, most of the companies did not have any formal means to deal with these concerns. One-quarter of the companies responding said that they provide spouse employment assistance and that their efforts are successful, in spite of difficulties in acquiring visas and work permits for the spouses, as well as in dealing with language barriers. Corporations' efforts include offering qualified spouses a job, introducing spouses to other companies, and providing money to spouses for résumé writing, language training, education, and cultural briefings. A few companies provide income replacement for the spouse for a designated period of time, although usually for only a few months.

Male Spouses in Corporations

As IN THE Foreign Service, the problems of male spouses of relocated businesswomen are garnering attention. Indeed, it has been suggested that the trailing spouse issue has only come alive as male spouses have begun to be affected. For example, a 1993 *Wall Street Journal* article entitled "Husbands in Limbo"[17] deals only with domestic relocations, yet the issues are familiar. While women accounted for only 5 percent of corporate moves in 1980, they now account for 18 percent of such moves. (The number of female expatriates was estimated at only 5 percent in 1992, according to the Windham International report cited earlier.) The husbands of these women, according to the article, "are finding themselves caught in an awkward sex-role reversal. The strain tends to intensify when a relocated husband can't find a new job and must depend on his wife's paycheck."[18] Some marriages cannot bear the strains and dissolve. Companies are concerned, as "they worry that they will lose prized fast-track women employees if career-minded husbands balk at transfers."[19]

The article cites negative attitudes toward husbands who follow their wives. Like the dependent male spouses of female Foreign Service officers, these men are in an unusual situation and are treated as aberrant. One man said that his friends were "aghast" that he relocated for his wife's job, and he said that following her felt like "losing part of being a man."[20] Others interviewed for the article posed questions relevant to the Foreign Service spouse problem, such as: "Is one career more important than someone else's? Or is someone else's career more important than the marriage?"

What Is a Spouse Worth?

THUS, WHILE a career in the U.S. Foreign Service affects one's spouse more than perhaps any other career, there are parallels between the problems Foreign Service spouses face and those of corporate spouses. Studies of military wives have also documented similar situations. Wives may still choose to make contributions as their husband's adjunct and define themselves primarily as the "wife of"; many still do, in spite of the modern denigration of this role. Dependent spouses overseas recognize that their role is a devalued one; for the men it is seen as deviant.

The problems of Foreign Service spouses, then, are no longer entirely unique but can easily be seen as common in present-day society. A clear illustration of this point is a recent divorce case between a top General Electric executive, Gary Wendt, and his stay-at-home wife, Lorna, which had newspapers and television news programs asking "What is a 'corporate wife' worth?"[21] The husband contested his wife's claim to exactly half of their assets, stating that it was he who had "worked," which entitled him to a much larger share. The wife argued that she deserves half to reflect her career as a "corporate wife": "decades of organizing GE dinner parties and trips abroad, giving other 'GE wives' tips on shopping and entertaining, and generally being 'the ultimate hostess.'"[22] She testified in court that she took this job very seriously. The judge awarded her half of the couple's cash, stocks, and other hard assets, but a smaller portion of her husband's stock options and future pension benefits. Thus she will receive less than the full half she demanded but more than the lump sum payment and alimony her husband had offered.

Researchers who study work and family issues increasingly argue that these problems cause stress and affect work performance, and employers who address these matters will be better able to recruit and retain the best workers and get higher levels of performance. From the discussion presented above, it is clear that U.S. corporations are acknowledging that when they plan for their employees they must also plan for their employees' families. The Foreign Service has been making efforts to help spouses find paying jobs at overseas missions. Perhaps the public and private sectors can assist one another so that families do not have to break up over the question of which is more important, marriage or career.

NOTES

1. Dick Buckley, *Report on the Role of the Male Spouse in the Foreign Service: A Survey of Experiences, Concerns, and Needs of Male Spouses Towards Foreign Service Life.* Unpublished paper sponsored by the Foreign Service Institute's Overseas Briefing Center, 1989, p. iii.

2. Ibid., p. 3.

3. Ibid., p. iii.

4. *New York Times*, "State Department: Till Reassignment Do Us Part?" (June 3, 1986), sec. B, p. 6.

5. These figures are from statistics provided by the Freedom of Information Office in the U.S. Department of State, Washington, D.C.

6. Rosabeth Moss Kanter, *Men and Women of the Corporation* (New York: Basic Books, 1977), p. 108.

7. Ibid., pp. 124–125.

8. Sue Shellenbarger, "Families Are Facing New Strains as Work Expands Across Globe," *Wall Street Journal* (November 12, 1997), p. B1.

9. Anne B. Hendershott, *Moving for Work: The Sociology of Relocating in the 1990s* (Lanham, MD: University Press of America, 1995), pp. 82–85.

10. Joann S. Lublin, "Companies Use Cross-Cultural Training to Help Their Employees Adjust Abroad," *Wall Street Journal* (August 4, 1992), pp. B1, B9.

11. Joann S. Lublin, "Spouses Find Themselves Worlds Apart as Global Commuter Marriages Increase," *Wall Street Journal* (August 19, 1992), p. B1.

12. Ibid.

13. Windham International and National Foreign Trade Council, sponsors. *Expatriate Dual Career Survey Report* (New York, 1992), p. 3.

14. Ibid., p. 13.

15. Ibid.

16. Ibid., p. 5.

17. Joann S. Lublin, "Husbands in Limbo: As More Men Become 'Trailing Spouses,' Firms Help Them Cope," *Wall Street Journal* (April 13, 1993), pp. 1, 6. This article also quotes Arlene Johnson of the Families and Work Institute, who suggests that the trailing spouse issue has only come alive as male spouses have begun to be affected.

18. Ibid., p. 1.

19. Ibid.

20. Ibid., p. 6.

21. Paul M. Barrett, "Wendt Divorce Dissects Job of 'Corporate Wife,'" *Wall Street Journal* (December 6, 1996), pp. B1, B8; 20/20, March 14, 1997.

22. Ibid., p. B1.

8

Should Foreign Service Spouses Be Compensated?

The story of Lucille Bloch has been in the news in recent years.[1] In 1989, Bloch's husband, a senior Foreign Service officer, was accused of being a Soviet spy; he was fired and his pension was withheld, but no formal charges were ever brought against him. Mrs. Bloch's life was turned upside down, even though she denied any knowledge of anything her husband might have done and no allegations were ever made against her by the government. For months she was tailed by the FBI. She lost her position of executive director of the American Austrian Foundation because of the publicity. When Felix Bloch was stripped of his pension and health benefits, so was she. She eventually divorced her husband and searched for a new job. As columnist Anna Quindlen wrote in *The New York Times* : "Lu Bloch considers that she was a hardworking State Department employee who has never done nor been accused of doing anything wrong, and that the least she deserves is her share of what would have been her husband's pension and health benefits."[2]

Mrs. Bloch was a traditional Foreign Service wife who performed her share of volunteer and representational work. Because her economic stability was tied to her husband's, his troubles led her into financial disaster. Many younger wives today fear that her plight could be theirs—because Foreign Service wives are so strongly tied to another person, they are placed in a very insecure state.

Moving Toward Compensation

To REMEDY this problem, many believe that Foreign Service spouses should be given their own pay and pension. In the United States, giving value to something usually means giving it a price tag, and some say that instead of the '72 Directive, which gave wives private status, wives should have received an official governmental role and a salary to go along with it. Paying spouses for the representational work they have traditionally done has been under consideration for over a decade. In 1984, a group of Foreign Service wives led by Marlene Eagleburger, wife of Under Secretary of State for Political Affairs and later Secretary of State Lawrence Eagleburger, presented to Congress a suggested pay amendment to the Foreign Service Act of 1980. This amendment proposed that spouses who agree to carry out representational activities be given a supplemental allowance of up to 40 percent of the employee's salary. The proposal pointed out that twenty countries already allow for such compensation. While Mrs. Eagleburger's plan was not adopted, it did renew attention to the situation of Foreign Service spouses, within and outside of the Department of State, and received press coverage.

Spousal compensation is still very much a live issue. The recording secretary of the Association of American Foreign Service Women (AAFSW), Christine Shurtleff, outlined a plan for spousal compensation in the January 1992 issue of the AAFSW newsletter. Shurtleff says that "The Foreign Service spouse has become an endangered species" because "the Foreign Service has been systematically losing its representative family make-up overseas as more and more employees are arriving at post as single (whether married or not)...."[3] This author asserts that spouses have always performed an important role, and that when they perform this role well they have an important positive influence on United States objectives overseas, while they also free employees to perform their jobs more efficiently.

Shurtleff suggests that those spouses who wish to perform "the spousal role pre-1972," or "the 'two for the

price of one' role" may voluntarily sign a contract with
the administrative office at each post and then be compensated for that role. Guidelines would be established
for evaluating spouses' performance. As examples of work
for which spouses should be compensated, she lists the
following:

> Help out with visiting delegations...; boost mo-
> rale at post by finding solutions to problems in-
> stead of complaining; respect local customs, learn
> local languages...; arrange proper representa-
> tional functions for the employee spouse and
> "work" rather than simply "attend" representa-
> tional functions outside the home; be aware of
> basic U.S. foreign policy and business interests
> in the host country and of local and international
> events that impact on those interests; create a
> warm, welcoming American home and treat all
> with whom s/he comes in contact with dignity
> and respect, demonstrating the charitable, giv-
> ing nature of Americans; take a leadership role,
> and be available to help less-experienced spouses
> cope with life overseas; enthusiastically embrace
> and attend community events.[4]

Shurtleff proposes two possible methods of payment.
The first option would be to provide spouses with half the
full-time salaries of lower-level officers, and have partici-
pants contribute also to social security. The other payment
option would be to add 25 percent of the employee's salary to his or her paycheck as an allowance for the spouse.
Payment would be provided only for the time the couple
is at post.

Barbara Frechette, a journalist, part-time mutual
funds salesperson, and the wife of an ambassador, has also
written about the issue of spousal compensation. In "Unwilling Unemployment,"[5] Frechette argues that the Foreign Service's reliance on volunteer support from spouses
has not diminished. Spouses especially help to foster a sense
of community at post. But, as Frechette points out, because fewer married officers are going overseas and more
spouses are opting to stay at home, there are now fewer

spouses at posts abroad, to the detriment of the overseas community and of families facing separation.

Many believe the solution is to make work available for spouses at embassies overseas. While the government's progress with creating job opportunities for spouses should be applauded, Frechette doubts that becoming a government worker is necessarily the ideal for everyone. She cites recent U.S. survey results that say that Americans are becoming more concerned with leisure and family than with work. Thus, Frechette argues:

> If the Foreign Service truly expects to reflect current American role models, it should continue to seek employment opportunities for a majority of spouses, who want and need jobs. It should also refurbish a role for spouses who find themselves in Foreign Service situations in which they cannot work. This refurbished role could also be used by increasing numbers of spouses who might wish to replace work with family and quality of life as their primary concerns while serving overseas.[6]

Hence Frechette recognizes that many spouses do want paid work, but also asserts that the traditional role of spouses is still useful and important; both types of spouses should be able to coexist.

In her article, Frechette also discusses women's clubs overseas as providing a network of support for spouses. Much of the logistical support work that had been done voluntarily through the clubs in the past has now become part of the job description of the community liaison officer at each post. However, CLOs generally do not have the resources to take over all of the clubs' functions. As Frechette told me in a personal interview, "We give one person a salary and then she has to go out and find volunteers, who are therefore exploited." CLOs do often have to solicit volunteer help from other spouses. Frechette argues that CLO offices should be expanded to create more paid positions for unemployed spouses. But "promoting the employed ideal with the same determination critics say we once used to force all women into the nonworking, traditional mold is, once again, trying to fit all spouses into one role. Having won the right to work, we must now avoid making it a sin not to."[7] Thus this wife, mother, and professional argues for more legitimate choices for Foreign Service wives.

Frechette outlined her latest thoughts on spousal compensation in an interview at her home. What we must do, she said, is to define all the functions that are valuable to the Foreign Service that spouses have traditionally performed, and then provide allowances to spouses to pay for those services. For example, leadership is one valuable function that spouses have traditionally performed in overseas communities, yet they have been abdicating this important role and instead seeking paid jobs in the embassy. Foreign Service wives traditionally were leaders, Frechette argues: they were role models in overseas communities, they represented the United States in the host country, and they also were leaders of the expatriate community. They had high visibility. She agrees with Shurtleff that spouses who perform these functions now should receive allowances, which would be added onto the employee's salary.

Other spouses I interviewed had various ideas for spousal compensation. One recommended that every year some fixed amount (such as $2,000) be taken out of the employee's salary and set aside in an interest-bearing account for the spouse, to be given to her (or him) upon the employee's retirement or a marital separation. (Divorced spouses are already given a share of the employee's pension, provided they were married for at least ten years.) Another wife suggested that family members be given more paid trips home to the United States and other similar benefits, in lieu of financial compensation. Others would like to receive their own pensions, in their own names. Pensions would of course be a financial boon and provide some degree of independence, and would also symbolize that the spouses' lives had been well spent in the Foreign Service and that their contributions were recognized.

One spouse has asserted that before compensation can be won, the '72 Directive that "freed" spouses must be repealed because it is a legal document and any compensation for spouses would run counter to it.[8] She finds it sad that efforts most recently made on behalf of spouses, such as the skills bank, have consisted of assistance for spouses who would separate themselves from the Foreign Service. Instead, she says, the focus should be on giving value—cognitive and monetary—to the spouse's representational role.

Compensation for Foreign Diplomats' Wives

IT IS widely known that the foreign services of some other countries pay spouses. In the mid-1980s, it was reported that the Thai Foreign Service required Thai spouses to perform representational duties and compensated them at thirty percent of the employee's pay.[9] The Finnish government is also known to pay spouses.[10] American Foreign Service wives tend to hold the Japanese Foreign Service up as a model for emulation; I was repeatedly told by my respondents, "Japanese wives are paid." However, according to the Japanese Consulate in New York City, Japanese spouses are not given a paycheck in their own name. All Japanese officers receive a base salary, plus an extra 20 percent of that base while they are posted overseas. A consular official stated that wives of diplomats often remain in Japan with their children, but if they do accompany their husbands to posts abroad, an additional 20 percent is included in the husband's paycheck—the compensation is not given in the spouse's name.

In recent years, the German government passed a regulation providing compensation for spouses of all government staff (not only diplomats) who are transferred overseas. Yet again the compensation is not paid directly to the spouse but is added to the employee's salary. In this case, an additional 5 percent of the employee's salary is paid to him or her, tax-free, with the recommendation that the money be placed in a pension fund for the spouse. A German embassy official explained that, as is the case in America, many spouses are well-educated professionals who have to suspend working while they are abroad, including in the United States, as there is no bilateral work agreement between the two countries. He called the compensation a means, however small, to acknowledge the contribution of spouses. Yet if economic independence is what spouses desire, neither the German nor the Japanese arrangements are a step towards that.

The role of diplomatic spouses in other countries appears identical to that of American spouses. The English-language Israeli newspaper *The Jerusalem Post* reported over a decade ago on many of the same representational issues and spouse-related problems addressed here. The journalist who wrote the article described the wife's role in the following familiar way:

> The wife has to be witty and charming, wise and all-knowing, for one wrong word may make headlines—abroad or in the Israeli press. She has to be decorous at all times, and speak as many languages as possible. She is expected to attend with great interest boring exhibitions of unknown local artists, to sit through lengthy conferences on subjects she doesn't care about and in languages she doesn't understand. Afterwards she has to find the right words to congratulate the artist or the speaker.
>
> If she doesn't do "her" job properly, the diplomat's wife comes under a heavy barrage of criticism—from the embassy staff, from the local Jewish community or from visiting firemen. She is often told that the career of her husband depends on her performance.[11]

The discord between the different generations of wives is not unique to the American Foreign Service. An article about the British Foreign Office, "Why the Good Life Is Foreign to Diplomatic Wives," printed in *The Daily Telegraph* in 1987, reported that

> Old-style wives who loved the entertaining and its allowances mind bitterly when these disappear on their return and their standard of living drops. And they feel threatened by the new-style graduate wives who talk about work all the time, which older wives feel devalues what they have spent a lifetime doing.[12]

The wife of a German Foreign Service officer, who had been a Foreign Service officer herself, wrote in 1981 that unrest similar to that of the American wives arose in the 1960s among German diplomats' wives.[13] Because by the early 1970s the majority of wives were educated, qualified professionals who did not want to give up their careers and personal economic security, the divorce rate among diplomatic couples climbed.

Clearly, the themes and issues raised in the last several chapters are relevant not only to America but to other countries as well, and American spouses have looked to the compensation systems of other countries for guidance.

The AAFSW Report on the Role of the Foreign Service Spouse

THE DEBATE over compensation for Foreign Service spouses was addressed in a large-scale survey of spouses conducted in 1985. The majority of the respondents said that they should be compensated in some way: just over a quarter said they should be paid for their expenses, a smaller proportion said they should be paid for their expenses and time, and another quarter said they should receive a salary for their social support services. While some said they would feel like servants if they were paid, others said they felt like servants anyway. Some said they would be embarrassed if host country nationals knew they were being paid to entertain them; others argued that they perform a job for the U.S. government for which they should be paid. The authors of the study found that over half of the spouses surveyed said they would be willing to make a commitment to an official representational role in exchange for compensation.

The Older Generation's Views on Pay for Spouses

ALL OF the women interviewed for this book were asked if they thought they should have been paid for their Foreign Service work over the years. About half of the older women believe that pay for spouses is a good idea and should be implemented. For example:

> Well, there's justification for that. If there were
> not a wife, somebody has to turn up to do those
> jobs, somebody has to do that endless amount
> of work! Answering notes, and making out in-
> vitations. Responding to all the charity requests.
> Meeting all these people and accepting calls and
> returning calls. And having endless people to
> luncheon. (Jean)

So they feel that the amount of work that needs to be
done justifies compensation, perhaps especially for the
wives of high-ranking diplomats. That special assistants
may be hired for ambassadors who have no wife at post,
or for women ambassadors, proves the point. Margaret,
who is not an ambassador's wife, speaks of the value of the
work of the ambassador's spouse, and that it is still seen as
woman's work:

> My resentment, and I use the word *resentment,*
> came when we were living at post, and I noticed
> that the female ambassador brought in an assis-
> tant, fully paid by the U.S. government, with her
> own house and car, and with a husband, who
> came over and basically ran that embassy. She
> became the de facto Mrs. Ambassador. Though
> that ambassador, she had a husband. And I was
> offended by that. Because this was not a house-
> keeper, they had a housekeeper, this was really in
> fact a Mrs. Ambassador. And I became offended
> by that because I thought to myself, if they can
> do that, then every ambassador's wife should be
> given a salary like that.

Still, most of the older wives said they were opposed
to pay for spouses, either because it is not feasible or real-
istic or because it would send a bad message to the American public, or both. Sophie, who has been very involved
with this issue, said,

> I think it's a loser. We took it to the Hill, we
> floated it around the United States, and it got
> nothing but negative publicity. And it reinforced

the image of the Foreign Service, which I think is a false image, but nonetheless, the cookie-pushing image. And the whole thing is that wives of congressmen don't get paid. Wives of university presidents don't get paid. Wives of ministers don't get paid.

While it is a good point that these other wives (or spouses) might demand to be paid also, others brought up the issue that makes the Foreign Service unique: periodic moves and overseas living, which mean sacrificing a normal work life in the United States. Still, Elaine, one of the youngest of this group, stated forcefully that women should know what they're getting into when they marry a Foreign Service officer, and that wives are no longer required to perform any work:

> I can't say I'm in favor of [pay for spouses]. And I feel like I'm sort of betraying other women in the Foreign Service by feeling that way. I knew we were coming into the Foreign Service when I married my husband. And I have made the Foreign Service a part of my life, I enjoy what we've been doing overseas, and we have been able to call the shots completely in terms of how much I want to be involved in the embassy, in entertaining and all that stuff. And I would feel much differently about it if I were being paid to do what I do when I'm abroad. It wouldn't feel the same, and I would feel a greater obligation to do more, or maybe do it differently, be more professional about it. As it is, I do what I do because I want to do it and it feels right, without anybody pressuring me to do it.

The Newer Wives' Views on Compensation

TWO-THIRDS OF the younger wives were in favor of paying spouses, although many of them qualified their approval. For example, some said that they loved the idea but it would never happen. Others supported pay for spouses only if each spouse could choose whether or not to take the work—and the pay. Some said that while they were in favor of spouses being paid, they would not themselves choose to perform the work, even with pay. In contrast, three women were absolutely opposed to any proposal for paying spouses, and two were unsure. Two others said that spouses should not be paid a stipend or salary but should have their own retirement benefits or some other extra compensation. Perhaps the strongest, and simplest, remark on the issue of pay for spouses is the following: "If someone expects me to do something, they better damn well expect to pay me for it" (Rachel). This attitude is in stark contrast to the attitudes of many of the older wives, as described above.

Two wives brought up Hillary Clinton, drawing a parallel between their role and hers:

> In the State Department spouses fought for years for their performance not to be reflected upon their spouse, on the employee. But now that we have that, thank you very much, we have Hillary Rodham Clinton, who's working for free! (Kim)

> So yeah, I think certain levels of spouses should be paid for what they do. I think the President's wife should be paid for what she does!... But I don't see spouses getting paid when the President's wife doesn't get paid.... There's still this sort of attitude in the State Department about, "You should be grateful for everything you get!" (Amanda)

Unlike Foreign Service wives, the First Lady has a finite term for her role, and it happens that this First Lady in particular will have no problem resuming her career.

Others considered that in our culture, being paid gives importance and value to work: "When you're getting paid, there's more to it than pay. There's a line between a serious thing and a less serious thing" (Beth). This is reminiscent of the older wives who felt that their contributions were dismissed once they were no longer evaluated on their husbands' performance reports. When the government said to them, in essence, we don't officially care what you do (as long as you do not bring discredit on the government), the more traditional wives felt that they were being told that their work was unimportant. Younger wives, who have grown up with the expectation of financial compensation for their labors, feel that, in general, if work is not paid for, it is not important.

Those who were against paying spouses realistically pointed out that funding would probably be difficult to come by:

> Well, I think we're already living in a society where every American hates government and hates government employees and especially hates the Foreign Service because they think we live high, high on the tide on their tax dollars...we have major problems at home, and they're threatening to take away our housing, and yet a bunch of wives are asking for—No! If you want money you get in the Foreign Service yourself. Or get a job. (Sarah)

Foreign Service officers and their families do receive free housing when they are overseas, which is the one benefit that many wives say makes this lifestyle still financially worthwhile. However, this perquisite recently has been under reconsideration. Others expressed the worry that money to pay spouses would have to come from existing benefits:

> My view is that for the ambassadors' and DCMs' and maybe the counselors' wives there should probably be some reimbursement or stipend or something. I mean, if you're a single ambassador and you have to hire a housekeeper to do all this stuff, then that person gets paid.... I guess the way I look at it is, yes, spouses should be paid, especially for the upper-level officers, if they're doing a certain amount of work. The reality of it is, there's no money. And the money should go into the housing, and the education

allowances and evacuation pay and things like
that that are in danger of being cut.... And those
are things that are going to make families want
to go or not want to go. (Sandra)

Mary, who at 44 is more traditional than the others in
this group, does not want pay for herself but would like to
be acknowledged as part of a team. She would like to see:

Instead of monetary compensation, more benefits where you are actually considered to be a
part of it.... That the retirement will forever go
to the wife, you know.... To me, things like that,
to make you feel that you were on equal foot-
ing, that your traveling overseas doesn't mean
you're uprooted, you leave your job, you have
no security, that the State Department, instead
of offering compensation, offers security in the
form of retirement.

From Mary and others, *security* is a word that I heard frequently in the interviews. Wives have concerns for their
own financial security, as they have relinquished some or
all of their economic independence by becoming Foreign
Service wives.
    Ann, who has been able to pursue her portable ca-
reer in the fine arts, was strongly opposed to paying spouses
because of what it would symbolize:

The pay, I mean, that's like welfare. I mean it's
this kind of barefoot and pregnant payment. And
I don't think it's going to help.

She said that instead of pay, spouses should be guaranteed
employment in the federal government when their husbands are posted in Washington, D.C. She also suggested
offering wives money for tuition to further their education, for the following reason:

There should be scholarships and grants. I think
somehow wives should be prepared for when

their husbands find some delicious little thing on the beach.... Because it happens all the time.

Still, another spouse's opinion was that once spouses acquire pay for themselves, they will then want even more:

> I don't know, it's got to be some kind of a system, because just paying the money won't be enough because what will happen is, then that will become usual and ordinary and then it will be like, "Well, I do this and if I do anything more than that, then I should be getting even more." But the problem with the recognition is very real, the problem is when you're expected to do certain things.... Where do you get your compensation? Who does recognize you for what you do?...If you don't feel like it's worth it, how long are you going to do it? You do it because you don't have anything else to do (laughs). (Christine)

As has been shown, wives take low-paying, uninteresting jobs, agree to give dinner parties and receptions, and volunteer with the women's group or at the school, because professional opportunities are lacking. Yet being paid for these traditional activities is not seen as an optimal solution.

Therefore, although two-thirds of the younger wives I spoke with said that pay for spouses is a good idea and is deserved, a large proportion also said that they would probably not take the compensation themselves. Some argued that it is only the older or more senior wives that deserve pay. It seems that, while the younger spouses appreciate how hard the older generation worked, they don't value the work itself, so that being paid wouldn't make the work desirable. A few from the younger generation find the traditional spouse role "offensive," and being paid for it probably will not change that attitude, at least for now.

A few wives said they would be happier if only a few simple, symbolic changes were made: stop calling them "dependent spouses" and stop treating them as appendages to their husbands. Indeed, the *Wall Street Journal*

reported in 1995, under the heading "Diplomatic Correct-
ness," that a State Department memo had been issued urg-
ing that Foreign Service "dependents" now be referred to
as "eligible family members."[14] While one hears the more
agreeable term "family member" in the Foreign Service these
days, "dependent" remains the official designation.

Conclusion

THIS CHAPTER has presented many different views on, and
ideas for, spousal compensation. Most of the spouses interviewed for this book, and most of those who participated
in the 1985 survey, support some type of compensation, in
principle, for some spouses, particularly the spouses of
higher-level officers. At the same time, most believe that
compensation is such an unrealistic goal that the question
is moot. If the U.S. government is closing down embassies
and consulates to save money, they say, it will not spend
scarce funds to pay spouses. Yet in cases where others are
hired to perform work that spouses commonly do, spouses
should be paid. And when wives and husbands have spent
their adult lives as part of a two-person career, they should
receive their own retirement benefits.

NOTES

1. Amanda Bennett, "Diplomatic Wife Lucille Bloch Wants Gov-
    ernment to Lift Its 'Indictment' of Her," *Wall Street Journal*
    (October 20, 1993), pp. A1, A7; Anna Quindlen, "A Woman
    Scorned," *New York Times* (January 29, 1994), p. A19.

2. Anna Quindlen, "A Woman Scorned."

3. Christine M. Shurtleff, "The Foreign Service Spouse: An Endan-
    gered Species," *Association of American Foreign Service Women
    News* (January, 1992), p. 5.

4. Ibid.

5. Barbara Frechette, "Unwilling Unemployment: Wandering the
    Halls of Overseas Life," *Foreign Service Journal* (June 1992),
    pp. 24–29.

6. Ibid., p. 26.

7. Ibid., p. 29.

8. Penne Laingen, letter to the editor in the *Association of American Foreign Service Women News* (February, 1992), pp. 3, 7.

9. Nancy Bartels, "Spouses in Other Foreign Services," *Foreign Service Journal* (March 1985), p. 27.

10. Ibid.

11. Michelle Mazel, "Israel's Unpaid Envoys," *Jerusalem Post* (February 16, 1984), p. 6.

12. Catherine Stott, "Why the Good Life Is Foreign to Diplomatic Wives," *Daily Telegraph* (September 30, 1987).

13. Wendelgard von Staden, untitled essay in *Diplomacy: The Role of the Wife*, ed. Martin F. Herz (Washington, DC: Georgetown University Institute for the Study of Diplomacy, 1981).

14. Ronald G. Shafer, "Minor Memos," *Wall Street Journal* (February 17, 1995), p. A1.

Conclusion

THE SITUATION OF FOREIGN SERVICE wives, and increasingly husbands, is a case study in the area of work and family problems. This book argues that a career in the U.S. Foreign Service affects one's spouse more than perhaps any other career. The "role of the Foreign Service wife," both past and present, has been described, including how that role was institutionalized in the Foreign Service, and how it has become ambiguous. Respondents from two different generations of Foreign Service wives have told how they have performed, or resisted performing, that role. It has been shown how attitudes toward the expected role of diplomat's wife have changed, placing these attitudes into a context which recognizes the importance of historical and social change.

The place of wives in America has changed dramatically over the past several decades. While once wives were confined to the private sphere of the home, wives, and American women in general, may now seek their fortunes in the world of paid work. Greatly due to the Second Wave of the American women's movement, women now have more choices about what to do with their lives, and fewer constraints. This change has many effects on both personal and institutional levels. Wives may still choose to make their contributions as their husband's adjunct, in the role of "unpaid partner" or "auxiliary worker," and define themselves primarily as the "wife of"; many still do, in spite of the modern denigration of these roles. More research is needed on the extent to which the role of "wife" is a primary source of identity for women today and to what extent it will be for those of the next generation.

Alternatively, women may create identities for themselves that evolve out of their accomplishments in fields other than the home or the family. For young career women, these identities may be established before they become wives and mothers. One type of role should not be viewed as more important than the other; what is most important is that women have the ability to choose the role they desire. The expansion of such choices has been both the result of and the catalyst for change.

This transformation of the personal—the increase in choices available to women today—creates the necessity for transformation on the institutional level. In 1972, Foreign Service wives demanded to be "set free." Currently, those in the upper echelons of the business and government sectors can no longer expect that when they hire an employee they are getting "two-for-the-price-of-one." In addition to doing without the unpaid labor they were accustomed to receiving, corporate employers cannot transfer their employees around the globe as they see fit. It can no longer be assumed that employees' spouses, increasing numbers of whom have careers of their own, will agree to such moves.

Both the government and corporations have begun to address these new arrangements, as individual couples have been developing their own strategies of adjustment. One such strategy is to become a "commuter couple," in which each party pursues his or her career-track position in a different geographic location. One or the other spouse visits the other; thus they are said to "commute." The authors of one study of commuter couples contend that commuting is only an extension of the trend toward increased individualism, "which emphasizes that each spouse's worth depends on individual achievements rather than on family membership."[1] For the couples studied by these researchers, their satisfaction with their marriage was predicated on their satisfaction with their individual work; in other words, these individuals were unable to be content with any aspect of their lives unless they were pursuing fulfilling careers.

The incidence of commuting has been increasing in the Foreign Service, a fact that is bemoaned by many. A Foreign Service psychiatrist is one of several people who have written about the importance of the presence of spouses to the quality of life at posts overseas.[2] While most do not wish to divide their families, some choose commuting as the least negative of their options. Here again, no alternative is perfect.

Other strategies of adjustment on both the individual and structural levels have been discussed here, such as proposals for the compensation of spouses, the increasing incidence of tandem couples, and the new programs corporations are instituting to accommodate the needs of their employees' families. What emerges from my interviews with the Foreign Service wives is that despite the many incremental changes that have been instituted, there still remains much dissatisfaction among wives and increasingly among husbands, also. Because the role of the wife was incorporated into the structure of the Foreign Service—incorporated into the very way American diplomatic activity has been conducted—it is very difficult to bring about real change. One hopes that the Foreign Service is unique in this respect (it is in many others) and that other places of work will have greater success in meeting the needs of families today. In doing so, they will also meet their own needs for a content and productive workforce.

There is one final note to add to this discussion regarding the place of wives in contemporary America. During the first term of the Clinton administration, there was some debate over the legal status of the First Lady, Hillary Rodham Clinton, particularly when she was conducting discussions about a national health care policy. When several groups of health care professionals filed a lawsuit calling for Mrs. Clinton's health panel meetings to be open to the public, lawyers for Mrs. Clinton argued that the First Lady is actually a member of the government who may therefore conduct secret task forces. A judge agreed, saying that "Mrs. Clinton was a full-time Government official, not a private citizen," and that "it was reasonable to treat the President's spouse as 'a de facto officer or employee' of the Government, even though she is not formally appointed and takes no oath of office."[3]

Thus the status of this important "wife of" was decided in the courts. A few years later, the courts affirmed the work of corporate wife Lorna Wendt. Perhaps, in overdue recognition of the contributions of wives everywhere, the status of "wife of" is finally being seen as a legitimate one.

NOTES

1. Naomi Gerstel and Harriet Gross, *Commuter Marriage: A Study of Work and Family* (New York: Guilford Press, 1984), p. 13.

2. Elmore F. Rigamer, M.D., Untitled article in *Diplomacy: The Role of the Wife,* ed. Martin F. Herz (Washington, DC: Georgetown University Institute for the Study of Diplomacy, 1981); Penne Laingen, untitled article in *Diplomacy: The Role of the Wife,* ed. Martin F. Herz (Washington, DC: Georgetown University Institute for the Study of Diplomacy, 1981).

3. Robert Pear, "Mrs. Clinton, Government Official," *New York Times* (June 27, 1993), sec. 4, p. 2.

Bibliography

Alt, Betty Sowers, and Bonnie Domrose Stone. *Campfollowing: A History of the Military Wife.* New York: Praeger, 1991.

Barrett, Paul M. "Wendt Divorce Dissects Job of 'Corporate Wife.' " *Wall Street Journal* (December 6, 1996), pp. B1, B8.

Bartels, Nancy. "Spouses in Other Foreign Services." *Foreign Service Journal* (March 1985), p. 27.

Bennett, Amanda. "Diplomatic Wife Lucille Bloch Wants Government to Lift Its 'Indictment' of Her." *Wall Street Journal* (October 20, 1993), pp. A1, A7.

Blancke, W. Wendell. *The Foreign Service of the United States.* New York: Praeger, 1969.

Buckley, Dick. *Report on the Role of the Male Spouse in the Foreign Service: A Survey of Experiences, Concerns, and Needs of Male Spouses Towards Foreign Service Life.* Unpublished paper sponsored by the Foreign Service Institute's Overseas Briefing Center, 1989.

Calkin, Homer L. *Women in the Department of State: Their Role in American Foreign Affairs.* Washington, DC: U.S. Department of State, 1978.

Callan, Hilary. "The Premiss of Dedication: Notes Towards an Ethnography of Diplomats' Wives." In *Perceiving Women*, ed. Shirley Ardener. London: Malaby Press, 1975.

de Beauvoir, Simone. *The Second Sex.* New York: Vintage Books, 1952.

Department of State Publication 9914. "The Foreign Service Family and Divorce." Washington, DC: U.S. Department of State, April 1992.

Department of State Publication 9883. "A Career in the Foreign Service." Washington, DC: U.S. Department of State, July 1991.

Enloe, Cynthia. *Bananas, Beaches, and Bases: Making Feminist Sense of International Politics*. Berkeley: University of California Press, 1990.

Family Liaison Office. "Family Liaison Office: Overview." Washington, DC: U.S. Department of State, May 1990.

Family Liaison Office. "Paper No. 2: Bilateral Work Agreements." Washington, DC: U.S. Department of State, December 1992.

Fenzi, Jewell. *Married to the Foreign Service: An Oral History of the American Diplomatic Spouse*. New York: Twayne, 1994.

Fenzi, Jewell. "The Great Divorce: Why the 'Hands-Off' Policy Did More Harm than Good for Spouses." *Foreign Service Journal* (June 1992), pp. 17–22.

Finch, Janet. *Married to the Job: Wives' Incorporation in Men's Work*. London: George Allen & Unwin, 1983.

Fowlkes, Martha R. *Behind Every Successful Man: Wives of Medicine and Academe*. New York: Columbia University Press, 1980.

Frechette, Barbara. "Unwilling Unemployment: Wandering the Halls of Overseas Life." *Foreign Service Journal* (June 1992), pp. 24–29.

Friedan, Betty. *The Feminine Mystique*. New York: Laurel, 1983. Originally published in 1963.

Gamarekian, Barbara. "Foreign Service Wives' Goal: Pay." *New York Times* (April 10, 1984), sec. A, p. 28.

Gerson, Kathleen. *Hard Choices: How Women Decide about Work, Career, and Motherhood*. Berkeley: University of California Press, 1985.

Gerstel, Naomi, and Harriet Gross. *Commuter Marriage: A Study of Work and Family*. New York: Guilford Press, 1984.

Gore-Booth, Lord, ed. *Satow's Guide to Diplomatic Practice*, 5th ed. London and New York: Longman, 1979.

Gotlieb, Sondra. *"Wife of"...An Irreverent Account of Life in Powertown*. Washington, DC: Acropolis Books, 1985.

Hart, Jane S. Untitled essay in *Diplomacy: The Role of the Wife*, ed. Martin F. Herz. Washington, DC: Georgetown University Institute for the Study of Diplomacy, 1981.

Hendershott, Anne B. *Moving for Work: The Sociology of Relocating in the 1990s*. Lanham, MD: University Press of American, 1995.

Herz, Martin F., ed. *Diplomacy: The Role of the Wife*. Washington, DC: Georgetown University Institute for the Study of Diplomacy, 1981.

Hochschild, Arlie. *The Second Shift*. New York: Avon Books, 1989.

Hochschild, Arlie. "The Role of the Ambassador's Wife: An Exploratory Study." *Journal of Marriage and the Family* 31 (1), pp. 73–87.

Kanter, Rosabeth Moss. *Men and Women of the Corporation*. New York: Basic Books, 1977.

Konek, Carol Wolfe, and Sally L. Kitch, eds. *Women and Careers*. Thousand Oaks, CA: Sage Publications, 1994.

Laingen, Penne. Letter to the editor in *Association of American Foreign Service Women News* (February 1992), pp. 3, 7.

Lederer, William J., and Eugene Burdick. *The Ugly American*. New York: Fawcett Crest, 1958.

Lublin, Joann S. "Husbands in Limbo: As More Men Become 'Trailing Spouses,' Firms Help Them Cope." *Wall Street Journal* (April 13, 1993), pp. A1, A6.

Lublin, Joann S. "Spouses Find Themselves Worlds Apart as Global Commuter Marriages Increase." *Wall Street Journal* (August 19, 1992), pp. B1, B5.

Lublin, Joann S. "Companies Use Cross-Cultural Training to Help Their Employees Adjust Abroad." *Wall Street Journal* (August 4, 1992), pp. B1, B9.

Mazel, Michelle. "Israel's Unpaid Envoys." *Jerusalem Post* (February 16, 1984), p. 5.

McCollum, Audrey T. *The Trauma of Moving: Psychological Issues for Women*. Newbury Park, CA: Sage, 1990.

The New York Times. "State Department: Till Reassignment Do Us Part?" (June 3, 1986), sec. B, p. 6.

The New York Times. "State Department: To Pay or Not to Pay the Spouse" (November 2, 1985), sec. 1, p. 7.

Ogburn, William F. "Cultural Lag as Theory." In *William F. Ogburn: On Culture and Social Change: Selected Papers*, ed. Otis Dudley Duncan. Chicago: University of Chicago Press, 1957.

Papanek, Hanna. "Men, Women, and Work: Reflections on the Two-Person Career." *American Journal of Sociology* 78 (4), pp. 852–872.

Pavalko, Eliza K., and Elder, Glen H., Jr. "Women Behind the Men: Variations in Wives' Support of Husbands' Careers." *Gender and Society* 7 (4), pp. 548–567.

Pear, Robert. "Mrs. Clinton, Government Official." *New York Times* (June 27, 1993), sec. 4, p.2.

Quindlen, Anna. "A Woman Scorned." *New York Times* (January 29, 1994), p. A19.

Rigamer, Elmore F., M.D. Untitled article in *Diplomacy: The Role of the Wife*, ed. Martin F. Herz. Washington, DC: Georgetown University Institute for the Study of Diplomacy, 1981.

The Role of the Spouse Committee of the Forum. *Report on the Role of the Spouse in the Foreign Service: A Study of Attitudes and Perceptions of Spouses Toward Foreign Service Life*. Sponsored by the Forum of the Association of American Foreign Service Women, 1985. Available from U.S. Department of State.

Russell, Beatrice. *Living in State*. New York: David McKay, 1959.

Schuck, Joyce. *Political Wives, Veiled Lives*. Lanham, MD: Madison Books, 1991.

Seidenberg, Robert, M.D. *Corporate Wives—Corporate Casualties?* New York: AMACOM, 1973.

Shafer, Ronald G. "Minor Memos." *Wall Street Journal* (February 17, 1995), p. A1.

Shannon, Elizabeth. *Up in the Park: The Diary of the Wife of the American Ambassador to Ireland, 1977–1981.* New York: Atheneum, 1983.

Shellenbarger, Sue. "Families Are Facing New Strains as Work Expands Across Globe." *Wall Street Journal* (November 12, 1997), p. B1.

Shurtleff, Christine M. "The Foreign Service Spouse: An Endangered Species." *Association of American Foreign Service Women News* (January 1992), p. 5.

Snyder, Nancy McCarthy. "Career Women in Perspective: The Wichita Sample." In *Women and Careers*, ed. Carol Wolfe Konek and Sally L. Kitch. Thousand Oaks, CA: Sage Publications, 1994.

Stone, Bonnie Domrose, and Betty Sowers Alt. *Uncle Sam's Brides: The World of Military Wives.* New York: Walker, 1990.

Stott, Catherine. "Why the Good Life Is Foreign to Diplomatic Wives." *Daily Telegraph* (September 30, 1987).

Sullivan, Margaret W. Untitled essay in *Diplomacy: The Role of the Wife*, ed. Martin F. Herz. Washington, DC: Georgetown University Institute for the Study of Diplomacy, 1981.

von Staden, Wendelgard. Untitled essay in *Diplomacy: The Role of the Wife*, ed. Martin F. Herz. Washington, DC: Georgetown University Institute for the Study of Diplomacy, 1981.

Weil, Martin. *A Pretty Good Club: The Founding Fathers of the United States Foreign Service.* New York: W.W. Norton, 1978.

Whyte, William H., Jr. "The Wife Problem." In *The Other Half: Roads to Women's Equality*, ed. Cynthia Fuchs Epstein and William J. Goode. Englewood Cliffs, NJ: Prentice-Hall, 1971. Originally published in *Life* (January 7, 1952), pp. 32–48.

Windham International and National Foreign Trade Council, sponsors. *Expatriate Dual Career Survey Report.* 1992.

Winfield, Fairlee E., ed. *The Work and Family Sourcebook.* New York: Panel, 1988.

Workman, James. "Gender Norming." *New Republic* (July 1, 1991), pp. 16–18.

Index